A NEW

JOURNEY

A New Journey

Samantha Kannan

Acknowledgements

This book wouldn't be possible if it weren't for several people. The first is my husband, Kannan, who always believed in me and supported my dreams. Without Joseph Sir and his school, I never would have had these experiences. They welcomed me with open arms, and I will always look back on that time fondly. To my colleagues and students, you made Kerala my second home, and I'll always remember you with love, especially Amal P for literally saving my life. I'd like to thank my friend Jurnee Clark for giving me permission to use her name, Dinil Devassy for introducing me to Kerala, and Sindhu Sriram, Mellissa Roemer, Vivek Nair, and Karthik Padmanaban for helping me with my preliminary edits. I'd like to thank Mystique Roberts for inspiring me to start writing and Jenna Moreci for her YouTube videos that provided endless insights into the writing process. Professionally, I'd like to thank Dhil Krishna for his brilliance in bringing my vision for the cover to life [instagram: @dhilkrishnadk], Brian Paone for his expertise and patience with editing [scoutmediabooksmusic. com], and Kari Holloway for her beautiful formatting [khformatting.com]. It would be a crime to not mention some of my biggest encouragers—the friends I've made online through Quora, Twitter, Instagram, TikTok, and YouTube. I'm forever thankful for your kindness and support, and I hope you enjoy reading my book.

FOREWORD

Where a New Journey Gives Birth to a New Life

It's truly a joy to write this foreword to A New Journey by Samantha Kannan. Life is a quest for moments of passion, connection, and love, and real success is the ability to share them. Life is a cycle of beginnings and endings, each ripe with gifts and interdependent with the other. This recollection of her often rocky love affair with India has re-inspired me to continue my journey steeped in love and admiration for India and its people and problems.

Sit, enjoy Samantha's wide-eyed "birth" into education and how she brings "life" to herself and others leading to endings and new beginnings. Where are yours?

About twenty years ago, I was a very successful educational administrator/businessman in the United States facing retirement. One day at MIT, I listened to late Former President of India, Dr APJ Abdul Kalam Sir, urging established educators with Indian heritage to return to our villages, nearly void of educational opportunities and hope. His message was simple and engulfed my heart. My retirement was an ending, but I was invited to a new beginning led by the years of experience in education. There was no turning back.

Education is the key to helping bring India to developed status, and I had the gifts to support my family of a billion people. I raised my hand in that auditorium without thinking. "I will go!" I burst out. Nearly two decades, three thriving village schools, and thousands of passionate students later, I share this message with others. They may be facing an ending in retirement, like I was, or a beginning, like Samantha was a few years ago.

Without the symbiotic relationships of youth and mentor, a village can't thrive. Where can you share a beginning or ending and reap the benefits of a life beyond your greatest dreams? Samantha came to me as a bright-eyed, curious, and eager young educator just out of college. She was open to the journey with me to create hundreds of socially responsible, educated, and passionate citizens of great character to lead India to a country with developed status.

Lead by some healthy fear, compassion, and an indescribable hope, she offers her beginning to India. Her goal is not to change India as she captures its deep, engaging and colorful traditions, its authentic desire to include outsiders in life and celebration, its respect for nature and its big heart in her memoir. Samantha is a leader among the many volunteers who have come in support of my mission and have left our youth just a little more inspired to live fully by finding their passion and passing on that fervor. Her story is a delightful inspiration to others also searching for purpose and community. It is her beginning in education, and it ripples through student after student as it joins with my ending, continuing a beautiful and rhythmical cycle. Begin, read on, and remember this. Endings are never permanent. Perhaps they are beginnings in disguise.

~ Dr. Joseph D. Fernandez,
Founder and Managing Director,
St. Joseph International Academy, Kumbalam

CHAPTER 1

With a final click, I sent off my resume. This was always the hardest part—waiting. It seemed I got a new rejection daily. Sitting defeated, I wondered if it was possible to go crazy from non-stop rejections. Would I ever get a job? Would I ever be able to move out? It had been five months since graduation, and I was losing my mind. I'd received rejection emails from probably every school within a fifty-mile radius and only had attended a couple interviews. With winter setting in, schools were hardly trying to hire anyone. Classes had started months ago.

I felt hopeless, like maybe I should have majored in something else. Maybe I wasn't meant to be a teacher. I had wanted to be one since childhood, but maybe I was wrong.

"Jurnee!" My mom called from downstairs. "Dinner!"

I didn't feel like eating, but it would be a much needed break. Luckily, it was pizza.

She doesn't waste a moment. "Any word on the job search?"

I shrunk back in my chair. "Got a new rejection." I forced sarcastic enthusiasm.

"You'll get the next one," my dad said encouragingly.

"I don't know. Maybe I should have majored in marketing or engineering or something."

"This is what you love. You'll find a good one eventually."

"Maybe."

"What about applying to be a substitute teacher to get experience and references or volunteering with some after-school programs? It would at least pad your resume."

This was the last thing I wanted to discuss. I know they were just trying to help, but they made me feel worse. These pep talks had lost their appeal months ago. My friends who I had tutored had gotten placements, but I had barely gotten interviews. What was wrong with me?

"I think I'll eat in my room," I said as I stood, plate in hand.

They briefly protested, but they knew I need to be alone. How much rejection could one person possibly take before they go crazy? I sat in bed, watching *The Office* for the thousandth time as I ate my pizza. It was my favorite show, and, since I'd seen it so many times, it required hardly any thought at all. It was the perfect comforting background noise.

What did I do wrong? I don't want to give up and work retail, like when I was in high school, but I don't know if I could handle another rejection. What if I did volunteering, like my mom had suggested? At least I would have something to distract me and get experience.

I browsed online, but most of the results were for art and music teachers for after-school programs. There was some need for ESL teachers, but they required a basic knowledge of Spanish. Maybe I should learn Spanish. I was officially hopeless with no leads. I would live in my parents' house forever and die alone. This was my fate.

I went downstairs to get some popcorn, but my mom was there too. "What are you doing up?" I asked her.

"Couldn't sleep."

I reached into the cupboard. "Same." I didn't feel like talking and started to go upstairs. I normally loved late night chats with her, but after months of rejection and failure, I just wasn't in the right headspace.

"Jurnee, wait," she called behind me.

I stopped where I was standing but didn't turn around.

"I think I found a solution for you."

I slowly faced her, not hopeful but curious.

"Do you remember our old friend Joseph? The Indian man who worked at Cambridge Public Schools with Grandpa?"

This was completely irrelevant. "And …?"

"He runs a school in India, and I emailed him after dinner last night. We discussed your situation, and he said if you'd like to come help at his school, you're welcome anytime."

"So, let me get this straight. You decided to just discuss my failures with a random family friend we haven't even talked to since I was in kindergarten? Did you also put an article in the paper? Do you have to announce this to everyone?"

Of every solution she could possibly have concocted, how was leaving the country the optimal choice?

"You could have a nice vacation to a new place, enjoy a warm winter, get some life experience and professional experience. It's a great opportunity."

Apparently, my failures were so shameful they wanted me to be on a different continent. I walked upstairs with my popcorn, wishing I could just sleep for a week. I knew I was probably just being dramatic and overreacting, but I felt like such a failure.

The way I saw it, I had four options. I could read, watch *The Office*, apply for more jobs, or try to sleep.

I decided to be productive and went online to look for jobs again. I didn't want to live so far away but expanded the search radius to one hundred miles. I was getting desperate.

I loved my hometown and really didn't want to leave, but it may be necessary. It wasn't big by any means, just about seventy thousand people, but it was home. My favorite people were here. My favorite restaurants were here. A Domino's sat just a half mile away! I would have to totally start over somewhere else.

Nothing looked good. I couldn't really afford to be picky, but, wherever I ended up, I wanted to be there for a while and actually build a career, not just use it as a steppingstone. Maybe I should give up my dream of teaching and find something else. If I went much longer without finding a job, my degree would be useless, and the next batch of graduates would be first in line. My clock was ticking.

I remembered my mom's recommendation of going to India. Maybe it wouldn't be totally awful. It would definitely give me a leg up. How many people could say they had volunteered teaching in a different country? Maybe it was worth a try.

I couldn't remember his last name, so I made the mistake of searching "Joseph School India." The result was a school for Native American children in South Dakota. I didn't want to ask my mom and admit defeat, so I searched her Facebook friends list instead. She was friends with four Josephs, but only one was Indian—Joseph D. Fernandez. I clicked his profile and saw mention of a school. This had to be him. I sent a friend request, and, to my surprise, it was accepted just a moment later.

He sent a message immediately. *Hello, Jurnee. Is this the daughter of Jim and Vanessa?*

Yes.

I spoke with your mother earlier. She mentioned that you may want to come to India to do some teaching and get experience before looking for a job.

Wait. She hadn't snitched on my failure? *That's correct.*

You're welcome to come anytime. We have our next term starting at the beginning of January, or you can come when we resume from summer break in June.

Could you tell me more about the facility? I wasn't sure what Indian schools were like and didn't want to agree to something without knowing every tiny detail.

We teach is kindergarten to tenth grade in a village setting. There are about three hundred students and thirty-five teachers and other staff. We have a hostel too.

My grandpa always spoke so highly of you and your success in Boston. What made you return to India? Why not enjoy your retirement here?

I was born in this village in 1939. I went to America for my studies and eventually made my way to a good position in Cambridge Public Schools. I earned my citizenship, got married and had six children, all of whom are now grown. Dr APJ Abdul Kalam, former Indian President, gave a speech some years ago to Indians settled in America and encouraged us to do more for our India. So, when I retired, I took my pension and decided to give back to my village by improving the education available.

Wow, that's amazing. I couldn't believe it. How does one person accomplish so much in their life? *How long were you in the US?*

Fifty years.

How much money does it cost to live there, if I were to come to teach?

You won't have any expenses while you are here. We will provide you with food and accommodation in our student hostel.

What would I be doing day to day?

I would like you to primarily speak with the younger students to improve their English speaking. You can repeat simple sentences with them, so they can internalize the American accent and tone.

It didn't sound too difficult. *Is there anything I should bring? Do you have Wi-Fi?* I felt a silly asking for Wi-Fi, but the internet was basically oxygen.

Bring anything you'll need for the duration that you'd like to come. I would recommend coming from January to the beginning of March, so you can be here for the full term, but it depends on your comfort. We do have Wi-Fi, so you should feel at home here.

It actually sounded promising. *Could you send me any photos?*

He immediately attached several photos. The school was massive and regal. Tan pillars stood tall in the front, surrounded by lush greenery and children standing in dark blue uniforms. The teachers stood beside, wearing beautiful dresses with extraordinarily long hair. It looked like heaven. Was this too good to be true?

If I did come, how would I do so? I haven't travelled before.

You'll want to decide soon, since it is nearly November. First, you'll apply for your passport and then Indian visa. Once you have the documents, you can book tickets from the beginning of January to the middle of March. Take ticket to Thiruvananthapuram, Kerala—also called Trivandrum, the capital of the state of Kerala. It is the closest airport.

How far are you from Thiruvananthapuram?

You can take a bus or train or hire a car if you are more comfortable. Prices are low here, since we are a developing country, so don't worry about cost of transportation. It will take probably two hours to arrive.

Let me talk to my parents and think it over. I'll let you know soon.

Sure. Take care, Jurnee.

I opened Google and searched for more about Kerala. It was called *God's Own Country*, and the images were breathtaking. It wasn't just the school; every place was green. There were beaches. There were giant boats in water. There were rolling hills and what looked to be tea plantations. It was almost too perfect; it couldn't be real.

I changed my focus from photos to reading, primarily about safety. Every site said it was among the safest destinations, especially for women, in all of India. I clicked everything and fell into a Wikipedia hole.

I awoke to my laptop on my face and my mother in the doorway. The sun shone brightly through my curtains. How long had I slept?

"I heard you spoke with Joseph last night. Does that mean you might want to go?"

"I don't know. I'm thinking about it."

"Well, if you decide to go or not to go, your father and I fully support you either way. We just want what's best for you."

"I know."

"Waffles?"

"Sure, give me a minute."

She went downstairs as I sat at my desk and opened my notebook. I should make a pros and cons list. That always solves everything.

Pros
- Get a break from rejections
- Get teaching experience
- Travel
- All costs are covered
- Once in a lifetime experience
- It's a beautiful place

Cons
- The only person I know, I haven't seen in about fifteen years
- What if no one else knows English
- What if the food is bad.
- What if it isn't safe.

I sat making notes for what felt like just a few minutes but, according to my father's increasingly loud knocks, was much longer. "Ready for waffles?"

"Coming, Dad." I closed my notebook and followed him downstairs.

We sat at the table, juice and water at each plate adorned with fresh waffles smothered in chocolate syrup and maple syrup—my favorite.

"So, Jurnee …"

Oh no. The serious voice. They even reached to hold hands. This was serious.

He took a deep breath and looked at my mom. "We think you should go to India."

Wait. Was this an order now? Was I being shipped off to India? Before I could start, he began, "We love you, and it's a great opportunity. You'll get to travel and learn more about the world and, of course, get teaching experience. At the very least, it'll look great for your resume."

It was no longer an offer; it was an order. I looked down and ate my waffles. This was why they wanted to make my favorite, because they were forcing me out of the country. I wanted to resist it, but I tried to be mature and recall my pros/cons list. I did have more in the pro column than in the con column.

"Fine. I'll go," I said with a sigh. I wasn't totally sure, but it didn't feel like this was debatable. And, after all, I had reached the same conclusion on my own. There was no sense in behaving like a petulant teenager.

They were a little too excited. "Really?"

I nodded weakly as I chewed my waffles.

"Oh sweetie, that's great. He said you were interested in coming from January to March. Is that correct? We should really get your passport soon then."

"Yes."

I ate my waffles in silence while they excitedly made plans for me—a little bit *too* excitedly. I excused myself and went upstairs. I wondered if any movies had been filmed in Kerala, so I could see more of how it looked. A quick Google search revealed that Kerala had their own movie industry, and their movies were on Amazon Prime. In the US? I saw one with good reviews called *Ohm Shanthi Oshaana* and clicked on it. Luckily it had subtitles.

The very first thing in the entire movie, even before the production company information, was TOBACCO USE LEADS TO CANCER with extremely graphic photos. What was this? Were they serious? Was this on all movies, or did this one just have excessive tobacco usage?

The first scene featured a motorcycle and cigarettes, so maybe the warning was appropriate. But then they claimed no one in the movie would smoke and that it was a bad habit. Weird, but it's a nice message. I wondered if smoking was common in India.

With that, the movie began. It was an amazing movie, and the lead actors were gorgeous. The girl was beautiful, but the boy was one of the most handsome people I had ever seen. I discovered that his name was Nivin Pauly, and I made note to try to watch another of his films, since I was apparently going to Kerala.

I really liked that the movie had such a sweet love story, where he wanted her to finish her degree instead of running off with him. I liked that it allowed the female role to take on more stereotypically masculine characteristics, like riding a motorcycle, being a doctor, and taking on the role of the pursuer in the relationship. I had only seen Hollywood movies before, but maybe movies and people from Kerala were just super progressive. At the very least, they were incredibly attractive.

I did a bit more research about Kerala online. It was apparently the cleanest state in India, the birthplace of Ayurveda, had the highest literacy rate, lowest corruption rate, and was even mentioned as a paradise on Earth by *National Geographic*. They had elephants and beautiful waters. Almost nothing seemed negative about Kerala, and I decided I was definitely going. I held a lingering fear about travelling abroad alone in a place that may not have many English speakers, but Joseph was a family friend. It would be okay.

Walking downstairs, I announced that I wanted my passport, and my mother immediately went to locate the required documents, so I could apply for it the next day. I was going to India. This was it.

The next few weeks went by fast. Getting my passport took just a few weeks, since we paid to have it expedited. Getting my visa took just a couple days and the completion of a two-page questionnaire. Then it was time to book the ticket.

We found one from Chicago to Trivandrum with a layover in Dubai. Since we were booking on such short notice it was about a thousand dollars, but I wouldn't really have any living expenses once I reached there so it seemed reasonable.

My parents booked it for January second to March sixteenth, so I could have a couple days to see Trivandrum while I overcome jetlag. I sent a message to Joseph with the final details. I had my ticket. This was really happening.

We read a lot about cultural norms and watched more movies to get an idea of how I should dress. It seemed like they dressed similarly to the way I do when they weren't wearing traditional Indian clothes—shirts and jeans. I could handle that. It seemed they wore sandals and flip-flops more than sneakers though, so I made note to buy some extras.

For Christmas, everyone bought me new luggage, new towels, some Kerala guidebooks, and Malayalam phrase books. New Year's Eve served as a goodbye party. All of my friends were jealous. They had gotten jobs already and were bound to their teaching contracts, whereas I was about to take a two-and-a-half-month-long trip across the world.

I had been jealous of them getting jobs, but now they were jealous that I didn't have one. It was strange how the tables had turned.

The total flight with layovers would be just over twenty-four hours. I couldn't even fathom travelling for twenty-four hours straight. It seemed so bizarre and made the Earth seem smaller yet bigger at the same time.

The morning of my flight arrived, and I packed the maximum fifty pounds. My dad put it in the trunk as I sat in the back seat with my backpack. It was a one-hour drive to the airport, then I wouldn't see the outside until I was in Kerala with the lush greenery and Nivin Paulys of the world. I had watched all of his biggest movies in preparation—*Premam, Bangalore Days, Action Hero Biju.* I was all caught up.

I looked out at the empty trees around me. Fully in the throes of winter, the trees were dark brown skeletons coated with shining white snow. Tomorrow everything would be green, and I would be warm. It was truly bizarre to think about. I didn't even bring a proper coat, knowing it would just waste luggage space.

We stopped in the airport drop-off lane, and my parents gave their tearful goodbyes with tight hugs and stern warnings to be careful and to keep them updated. It felt so strange to think I wouldn't be back for months. I would miss them greatly, but this trip could change everything for me. I'll finally be a teacher, maybe even a professional teacher when I return.

"I'm sorry about everything," I said.

They hugged tighter. "We know. We just want you to be happy."

With one last hug, we said our final goodbyes, and with a final deep breath of Chicago air, I entered the airport lounge.

CHAPTER 2

I stepped out of the airport, and everything overwhelmed me. Each sense took in so much more than I was accustomed to. I felt as though my fine, wavy hair had ballooned into a frizzy mess within seconds.

A constant chaotic bustle of horns, chatting, dogs, vendors, and taxi drivers shouting carried down the street. Everything overlapped until it became nonsense. It was late at night, but that didn't seem to put a damper on things.

I smelled an aroma I hadn't encountered before to this degree. It reminded me of the Nag Champa incense my cousin used to burn. It wasn't subtle though; it engulfed me. I could taste it.

The air was heavy. I felt the humidity and the heat, even at midnight, taking hold. Like a tight hug from an acquaintance I wasn't quite expecting, India welcomed me.

Anachronisms surrounded me. Women in *sarees*, men in *mundus*–but the younger generation donned jeans. It felt contradictory. The *sarees* and *mundus* seemed to be continuous lengths of fabric. *Sarees* were draped across the whole body before falling carefully over one shoulder, and *mundus* wrapped around the waist were paired with regular button-up shirts. New cars seemed to be everywhere, but old bicycles. The airport was new, but everything outside was old. I saw an old woman selling some kind of food from what looked to be a cart and was almost tempted until I remembered the advice cautioning me from eating anything sold outdoors. I was so hungry it would almost be worth the sickness though.

I saw palm trees. I'd never seen one in real life. Or was a coconut tree? I tried to remember the difference, but now seemed like hardly the time to consult Google. I wasn't sure where to begin. The lights were so bright I couldn't even see the stars. It was past midnight, but, to my jetlagged mind, it was lunchtime.

I grabbed my phone and ordered an Uber. "Feels just like home," I said with a chuckle. I remembered how excited I had been to know my TMobile sim worked in India at no extra cost for data or texting. I just couldn't make calls without Skype or Facebook.

A boy, no older than fifteen, asked if he could take a selfie with me. Why was he out so late? Where were his parents? I must've looked dreadful from the long flight, but I agreed. He took the photo and thanked me as he walked away. I looked around to see if anyone else had noticed. Did I resemble any Indian celebrities? I couldn't possibly, and I certainly didn't resemble any American celebrities.

I wanted to get to my Airbnb and settle in, but I was a strange mixture of wide awake and dead tired—tired from the flight yet awake from the excitement of a new place. I wanted to see everything, but it'd have to wait until tomorrow.

My phone alerted me that the Uber had arrived, and I looked around for it. Cars were everywhere. What was a Maruti Suzuki Swift Dzire? His name was Anooj. Should I say his name when I say hello to confirm it's him? What if I pronounce it wrong? What if I offend him, and then he leaves me in the middle of the street?

I tried to shush my anxiety as I walked to the rolled-down window. "Aanooj?"

"Anooj, madam. You are Joornee?"

"Jurnee," I corrected him, and we both laughed about our mispronunciations.

"Is this your first time to India?" He emphasized *India*, every syllable stretched out with pride.

"Yes."

His English was surprisingly good. I didn't think it would be this easy to communicate with people. A wave of relief washed over me.

"You must allow me to show you everything. Tomorrow, I can take the day off and give you a tour."

I was hesitant but intrigued. I would love to see the sights, but could I trust him? Sure, Uber did background checks in the US, but was it the same for India? Was it safe? Even if it was safe, it would be wrong to ask him to take the day off.

He noticed my concern. "Madam, please no worries. It is okay if you don't wish to come. I only want for you to see everything which my *India* has to show."

He seemed genuine, but I was still torn. It would be nice to have a local contact to help me get around and communicate more efficiently, but what if he was a psycho who preyed on solo female travelers?

"So, what do you do when not driving Uber?"

"I'm a software engineer."

I was shocked. "So Uber isn't your job?"

He laughs. "I wanted a car but didn't want a loan. I'm just doing it now for time pass to pay the loan faster."

It was genius.

We continued the drive in silence until we reached my Airbnb. The lights were on, and a massive cement fence surrounded it. Was that normal? It looked like a fortress.

Anooj handed me a piece of paper. "If you need anything, please call or send me a WhatsApp message anytime. *Atithi devo bhava.*"

"What?" I didn't catch the last part.

"WhatsApp is a free SMS app in your mobile. Download it if you don't yet have it installed."

"No, no. The last part."

"*Uh-tee-tee day-vo baa-vuh.* It was meaning that, in India, we consider the guest as equal to God. Anything you wish, madam, I will be happy to help."

I smiled and thanked him, making sure to pronounce his name as he had directed. That was such a sweet concept. India had definitely given me a good first impression. If everyone was like Anooj, this would be the greatest few months of my life.

He got out of the car to help me with my bags. He looked almost American with his dark skinny jeans and simple t-shirt. I had often heard Indians described as short, but he was tall. Running his hand through his shaggy black hair, I noticed a dark red string tied around his wrist. I wanted to ask him about it, but I didn't want to seem rude or nosy.

"Everything okay, madam?"

I chuckled at this. In my life, no one had been so formal.

"You really don't have to call me *madam*."

"Okay, Jurnee, ma'am. Your wish."

I rolled my eyes. "Just *Jurnee*."

"Okay, *Just Jurnee*."

I couldn't help but to laugh. These kinds of jokes annoyed me to no end at home, but it was kind of heartwarming when I was away. To think the same sense of humor was worldwide was incredible. I thought it would be so different here, but maybe, deep down, people were more similar than I had thought.

Anooj walked me to the cement fence and iron gate.

A man approached from behind it "Jurnee, Jurnee! Welcome to *India*!" he said with the same inflection over *India*.

Does everyone pronounce it like that? Should I also?

"I am Gopalakrish, but please call me as GK. I'm so happy you've come!"

"Thank you, sir." Names here were going to be hard.

As he reached to open the gate, Anooj turned. "Don't forget to ping me if you are interested in tour."

GK lifted my suitcase as I grabbed my backpack, and we entered. Inside the gate, the house was beautiful. Bushes of flowers lined the gate walls, and the ornate stone tiles of the driveway were incredible. The house was surprisingly green—not a dark, earthy green, like some were back home, but an actual bright green. I'd never seen a house this color. I wanted to ask about it, but I didn't want to be weird or rude, so I dropped it.

"You must be tired, dear. I will show you to your room, and we'll talk in the morning."

I nodded in agreement as we stepped onto the porch. Was it a porch? It wasn't wood but rather some kind of stone. Granite? Were granite porches a thing?

He removed his shoes, and I followed suit.

"Your house is beautiful."

He turned back and smiled, still leading me through the house. We passed through a cluttered living room full of at least ten seats and several display cases full of tiny statues. Up the stairs, he showed me a door to the terrace, the bathroom, and, finally, my room. It was small but more than enough. GK sat my bag beside the door and wished me goodnight. I honestly had no idea how he'd carried that monstrosity up the stairs, but I was thankful.

Sitting on the bed, I reflected on the past couple days. I had left my home, flown alone across the world alone to India, made my first friend, and now was at the place I'd call home for the next couple days. This was, hands down, the most exciting and uncharacteristic thing I'd ever done, and I was equal parts excited and petrified.

I wanted to sleep, so I could normalize my sleeping pattern and combat the looming jetlag, but I was too excited. I downloaded WhatsApp and opened Google to find some activities for tomorrow. I recognized it all from my previous searches, but I still couldn't decide. I found a beach, a zoo, and so many temples. I'd love to see a temple, but I don't want to disrespect anyone by accidentally doing something wrong or by entering as a nonbeliever, so I nixed it.

As much as I loved planning, I eventually decided to head to the beach and then just explore. *This will be so much fun*, I thought as I walked to the bathroom to clean up before sleeping. But, when I got to the bathroom, I reached a level of confusion I'd never had before.

There was no shower curtain. There was no partition. Instead, I saw only a hose on the wall. And a spicket. And a bucket? There was no toilet paper. A kitchen sink sprayer replaced where the roll should be. What kind of a bathroom was this? It was just an open room full of hoses and faucets. A big box sat beside what I assumed was the shower hose, but I didn't know its function. I felt so exhausted and overwhelmed I wanted to cry. I could already feel that heat behind my eyes. I knew it was coming, but I tried to stop it.

With hands on the sides of the sink, I closed my eyes. "Keep it together, Jurnee. This is not America. This is a different continent. Not everything will be the same as home." I looked at myself in the mirror for the first time in over thirty hours and immediately splashed water over my face to remove the shiny oil buildup and fallen mascara. *You'll figure out the shower after you've had some sleep*, I thought as I settled for trying to rinse myself with water from the sink.

I went back to my room, changed into clean pajamas, and crawled into bed. It was a little firm, but it had been so long since I'd been in a bed that my appreciation won out. With a deep breath, I tried to relax. It was just the stress making me so negative; everything was totally fine. Tomorrow would be my first full day in India. Tomorrow, I'd get to see everything. Tomorrow would be absolutely incredible. Most importantly, however, tomorrow would be the day I figure out how to take a shower.

Du-du-doo-doo-doo. Du-du-doo-doo-doo. The sound of my phone ringing awakened me. I opened my eyes to turn it off, but the sun was so bright I couldn't. Fumbling with the sides, I eventually found the lock button to silence the ring and breathed a sigh of relief. Nuzzling my head into the pillow, I tried to find sleep again, but it evaded me.

10:30. Only six hours of sleep. I wanted more, but I didn't want to waste the day. Ignoring the Facebook notifications, I checked my texts and calls—curiosity and excitement from friends, Anooj wishing me good morning, and my mom thinking I was dead.

I braced myself for a lecture about how I should have called or texted, about how worried she was, about how I was in a different hemisphere and anything could have happened. I replied to her thousand texts, *I'm alive. Just woke up. Everything was fine.*

She immediately replied, *Good. Be safe. Don't forget to give us AT LEAST a daily update, so we know you're okay.*

I replied to this and some other messages from friends, but soon the time had come to conquer the shower … with some help from Google.

After just a few minutes of scrolling and attempting different search queries, I realized most of the search results were about buying a shower heater in India or taking a bucket bath. Anooj and I weren't quite at that level of friendship to ask such questions, so I was in this on my own.

Approaching the giant white box, I noticed no buttons, knobs, or switches. I searched everywhere for something resembling a controller. Could there be a remote? After what seemed like an eternity, I found a piece of masking tape above a switch outside the bathroom— *Water Heater.*

I silently cursed myself and switched it on. A light on the box illuminated. Victory! It would probably take a few minutes, so I spend the next few minutes browsing my phone.

Anooj again. *Jurnee, I took leave today. Would you like me to take you for tour?*

No, thanks. I think I'll just relax and roam around. Another time.

For a moment, I could see him typing, but then he stopped. Then he started and again stopped. For a second, I felt guilty. Was it rude of me to say no?

I disregarded it and attempted to shower.

After learning how to turn on the hot water, it was a pretty normal experience. I got ready with my favorite maxi skirt and some bangles to blend in and headed downstairs.

"Good morning, GK."

"Jurnee!" He looked startled. "I wasn't expecting you to be awake so soon! Aren't you feeling jetlagged?"

"No, no. I'm fine. Why waste time, when there's so much to explore?"

"That's the spirit, dear. Do you want to eat at home, or were you thinking to have outside?"

"I wanted to eat out, actually. Could you recommend any place?"

"Ariya Niwaas. You must go to Ariya Niwaas. It's actually not far from here, and you'll love it. Very good and hygienic but not expensive."

"Great! Thanks so much, GK!"

I noted the directions and set out for the first day of my adventure. I'd have some breakfast and relax then maybe go to the beach nearby or shopping. The possibilities were endless, and I was certain this was the best decision I'd ever made.

I put on my sunglasses and walked through the gate, still uncertain of why it was necessary to have a giant cement fence. Trees grew everywhere, people walked here and there, an obscene amount of honking, some dogs, and more motorcycles and scooters than I'd ever seen before—sometimes an entire family on a single scooter. Everything was so beautiful and so different than anything else I'd seen before. I was completely awestruck but confused how I was the only one wearing sunglasses. It was so bright!

I continued walking toward the restaurant but noticed everyone staring at me. I really must've looked like a celebrity. First, the selfie kid at the airport, and now this, or maybe I just looked way more disheveled than I had thought. I tried to ignore it, but I felt more and more self-conscious.

"Jurnee," I silently scolded myself. "Calm down. No one was staring at you. You're just being paranoid. Stop it now."

Finally, I saw the white building, Ariya Niwaas. It was breakfast time.

I entered, and it resembled a normal American restaurant. All the other restaurants I had passed were outside with a few chairs or were simple looking with all open windows. This one looked like any I would see at home. *I bet that's why he sent you here. He thinks you can't handle a normal restaurant in India.*

"No, Jurnee." I tried to reason with myself. "He just wants you to be safe and not get sick. Don't overthink things."

I sat in a nice booth alone and read through the menu. Suddenly, I realized I didn't know what anything was. I looked around and saw a lot of people with something that looks like a fluffy white cylinder, some with thin rolled pancakes, and some with brown doughnuts. A panic came over me. *Why didn't I research Indian breakfast foods before coming out?*

Luckily, my waiter sensed my distress. "Madam? Ready?"

"No, I'm sorry. I don't know what anything is."

"No problems, madam. Tell what you like. You want healthy or spicy or little sweet?"

"Not super spicy but maybe a little."

"Okay, madam. I have the perfect thing for you. I will bring for you *masala dosa* with *sambhar*, tomato chutney, mint chutney, and coconut chutney."

"Sounds great." I smiled and thanked him despite having no idea what those words meant except for *tomato*, *mint*, and *coconut*. I'd never felt so relieved. How would I manage if I couldn't even feed myself? This would be so much more difficult than I had thought.

My phone chirped. *Hello, Jurnee. Had your breakfast?* Anooj was very persistent.

Yeah, just ordered. Will have it soon.
Great! What are you having? Any Indian dish?
Some kind of dosa. But it hasn't come yet.
Send the photo when it comes.

Scanning the restaurant, I saw it really was quite similar to restaurants back home. Ornate wooden pillars, big windows, and beautiful wooden chairs adorned the establishment. I didn't really feel like I was outside the US; it felt just like home.

As I waited for my breakfast, I quickly braided my hair. Indian humidity was more powerful than all of my hair products combined.

The *dosa* came, and it was even bigger close up. I had no idea any food existed of this particular size. It was nearly as long as my arm and felt less like a pancake and more like a crepe. The potatoes inside made it the perfect combination of everything I loved. And it came with soup and three sauces? How did this even work? I took the picture and sent it to Anooj. I posted it to Facebook too, since everyone wanted updates.

I tore the *dosa* and dipped it into the sauces and soup like I would with tortilla chips into salsa. I loved it, but I felt like I was definitely not doing it right, because my waiter returned to the table.

"Madam, do you want any help?"

Embarrassed, I nodded yes. Time for a *dosa* tutorial.

He looked to me with a questioning nod, I assumed asking permission to touch my food. I nodded in approval as he reached to my *dosa*, tore off a piece about four square inches, used it to pinch a large quantity of sauce, then finally dipped it into the bowl of soup and ate it. All with just one hand. I wondered if he was injured or purposely didn't use his left hand while eating.

It looked extraordinarily messy, but I gave it a shot. It tasted better this way, though my hands were now filthy, and I instantly regretted it.

He noticed my discomfort and gestured toward a washroom.

I thanked him and excused myself to wash my hands. When I returned, I resumed eating it like tortilla chips. I didn't care if it was wrong, at least it was less messy.

The bill was only eighty rupees—barely more than a dollar—and couldn't possibly be correct. I didn't notice the price on the menu, but surely it must be more than that.

I called for the waiter and pointed to the bill. "Is this an error?"

"No, madam. Eighty rupees only."

I was shocked, but I gave him a hundred and told him to keep the change. That's what we do in the US, but he protested. "Madam, no tips needed."

This was truly a different universe. He brought me the change, and I left, ready to explore the city.

I decided to not use Uber this time and take a rickshaw, so I could get a real feel of the city through tiny yellow and black cars with three wheels and no doors. I was fascinated by them as I approached the long line and bent to the first one. "Do you speak English?"

"*Illa*, madam."

Does that mean no? I walked down the line, asking each one until one finally said yes.

"Where you want to go, madam?"

"What do you recommend?"

The beach looked good online, but no one knew like a true local. Unless, of course, he drove me all over town just so he could charge me a ton. Maybe it was a mistake to let him choose. Or he could be dangerous. I should have asked Anooj. He was really nice and would have been great for showing me around town. It was too late now though.

"Do you want to see the beach?"

I agreed. I didn't, however, realize it would be a forty-minute ride. After about twenty minutes, I checked Google Maps every five minutes to ensure he wasn't trying to kidnap me.

All the bouncing destroyed my back by the time we arrived. We stopped, and the meter read five hundred and fifty rupees. Not even eight dollars for a forty-minute ride? This was heaven. I reached in my wallet to take six hundred to include a tip. Could we tip drivers at least? He took a lot of trouble to drive me; it was the least I could do.

Handing him six hundred rupees, he stopped me. "Madam, meter was broken. Rate was one thousand rupees."

That was just extortion. "I'll give you no more than seven hundred." I knew he was still taking too much, but I would never give him a thousand when the meter said five fifty.

"Rate was one thousand rupees. You will pay one thousand rupees."

"Seven hundred or I walk away." I may be naïve but not that naïve. It wasn't a lot of money, but it was wrong of him to try to cheat me like that. I'd read about people overcharging foreigners, but hadn't expected it to happen to me.

He shouted and everyone turned to look. Humiliated, I thought about paying him the full amount, but being charged double was where I draw the line. Out of the corner of my eye, I saw someone approaching and turned to see Anooj.

"How did you know I was here?" I whispered, shocked. It wasn't a huge beach, but it was a very bizarre coincidence. Then again, almost the entire beach was watching this scene unfold, so it would have been difficult for him to miss me.

"Just a minute. Go and sit there. I'll come in a minute." He pointed to a nearby bench.

"But I have to pay first."

"Wait there. I'll manage it."

Talk about just in the nick of time. I walked to the bench as I heard them shouting behind me. I had no idea what they were saying, but it sounded like Anooj was winning.

After a few minutes, he returned.

"What happened?"

"Why did you take an auto? You knew I would take you anywhere you needed."

"*Auto*? You mean *rickshaw*?"

"Most of us call them *autos*, but why did you take it? You could have called."

I shrugged. "I wanted to get the genuine experience."

"Autos are great for short distances. But, when you take one, you want to confirm the rate before you start or book online through Ola Cabs to get a confirmed rate before booking the auto. This is not America, Jurnee. You have to be cautious."

"So, what happened?"

"He charged you more because you are a foreigner. When you told no, he was surprised and became angry. I paid him the cost of the fare."

I reached back into my wallet to repay him, but he stopped me. "Friends do not accept payments from friends."

I was shocked. I had friends for fifteen years who would remind me about five dollars, and he barely knew me.

Changing the subject, I asked him, "So what are you doing here?"

"Came to relax. I love Kovalam Beach. I've been coming here since I was a kid, and it's my favorite place. I try to come every day if I can."

I looked around. It wasn't difficult to see why this was his favorite place. People were having fun everywhere, but ironically, no one was swimming. They would stand in the water, boat in the water, run near the water, shop and eat near the water, but actually swimming in the water? Apparently not. And no swimsuits.

"Why is no one swimming?" I asked him as we walked down the beach.

"It isn't safe. The current is very unpredictable, so we don't swim."

I guess it made sense, but it still made the beach useless.

"So, how was your *dosa*?"

"Great! Way messier than I had expected, but it was delicious."

"Messy?" He was confused, so I explained the tortilla-chip-dunk method versus the waiter's pinch-and-grab method. After I explained, he burst into explosive laughter. "I'll show you tomorrow. Don't worry."

I smiled. Anooj was my guardian angel of *autos* and *dosas*.

"Ready to go?" he asked as we continued walking down the beach.

"Where to?" I still wasn't sure if I should trust him all the way. After all, he was the one who said I should be more cautious. There was something about him though. I just felt like I could trust him. He seemed so genuine.

"I can take you to a lighthouse, a zoo, a theme park, a temple, a mall, an island. Anything you want."

"There's a lighthouse?" I had never seen one before and didn't remember seeing that online.

"Of course, come this way." He pointed just ahead. "It's just a few minutes' walk."

It looked unreal. I reached for my phone to take some pictures but paused. Would he think I was one of those annoying tourists who just takes pictures of everything? "You don't mind, do you?" I held it up to take a picture of the lighthouse with the beach in the background.

"Not at all. You clicking photos means that you are liking my Kerala. Click every photo you like."

I smiled. This place was incredible. I'd never seen anything so beautiful and didn't even know any place could look like this. The movies didn't do it justice. We walked around for a while and decided to wait in line to enter the lighthouse.

The long line gave us more time to talk. We discussed everything and nothing—trivial things, like our favorite foods; important things, like our families; deep things, like our thoughts on the universe. We never stopped talking, even for a minute. I wasn't sure what made me be so open with someone who was practically a stranger, but he was just so easy to talk to. Were all Uber drivers like this in India? I'd never had a conversation with one in the US.

I found out that he wasn't actually from Kerala though. He was from nearby Tamil Nadu, which apparently spoke a different language. When I expressed shock, he told me India had over a thousand languages. How was that even possible? His grandpa alone knew five languages. It was mind blowing.

"So, what brings you to India?" he asks.

Oh no. I took a deep breath and bared my soul. I told him about my struggles to find a teaching job after graduation, how I had felt like I was letting everyone down, and about the school I was going to soon. I was embarrassed to have shared so much with someone I didn't know well and expected awkward pity, but he didn't pity me or even try to give me another hopeless pep talk.

"That happens really often here. Every year, millions graduate, and there simply aren't enough jobs. It happened to me also."

"How did you deal with the constant rejection? How did you get your job now?"

"You just have to keep going. It's hard, and I also felt like a disappointment, but one day, I got an offer. Your time will also come."

"How long did it take you to get a job?"

"Almost two years."

I couldn't believe it. If he could make it through two years, I could manage a bit longer.

"Don't give up, *da*. Everything happens in its own time." He was saying the same things dozens of people had told me since graduating, but it meant more from someone who had been there.

Finally, we reached the top, and I took hundreds of pictures, but random people kept asking me for selfies. I thought the one yesterday had been a fluke. Was this a normal occurrence? It was nothing compared to the stares though. They were never ending, and it felt like they pierced my soul. I hoped it wasn't making Anooj too uncomfortable.

"So, what would you like for lunch in our Kerala?"

The jetlag was hitting me, and I had no idea where to even begin with food. I gave him a blank stare.

Luckily, he made a suggestion. "Have you had *parotta* before?"

"Par who?"

"*Parotta*. It's like a flat bread served with curry."

"Sure. Sounds great."

We walked to the parking lot, but I didn't see his car. Instead, we approached a motorcycle. "You have a motorcycle *and* a car?" I was shocked. Back home, it was a big deal to have both.

"The car is for my future family." He handed me the helmet. "I like my bike more."

"Congratulations!"

He seemed confused. "For what?"

"Your future family. I didn't realize your wife was pregnant."

His confusion increased tenfold. "No one is pregnant. I'm not even married. I just like to plan ahead."

I felt like a complete buffoon for this, and for realizing he only had one helmet. "But what about you?" I asked, gesturing to the helmet in my hand.

"I'll be fine. You be safe."

I had never been on a motorcycle and was terrified. At least traffic was slow, so no one would immediately run me over if I fell off, though I wouldn't mind entirely after making a complete fool of myself.

He brought us to a street food vendor. I couldn't eat here. It wasn't safe. I had read so many articles about food contamination. I must have the worst poker face, because he easily read me again.

"Okay, Jurnee. This is how you know when it's safe to eat street food. There's just one rule. There must be a line."

"A line?" That's it? The internet made it seem so much more dangerous and complicated.

"If there's a line, the food will definitely be tasty, because everyone likes it. It'll be fresh, because everyone is buying it. And you can watch them make it in front of you to see how clean they are and make sure nothing is raw. It's only the raw food that you want to worry about, because it has water in it."

"How do you know all of this?"

"My cousin owns a tour company, so he is around foreigners a lot."

We order *parotta* at the counter. The texture was unlike anything I'd ever eaten, kind of like an elastic *naan*. The curry contained potatoes, but I didn't catch the name. I loved it though.

"This is the best thing I've ever eaten." I took pictures to send home.

"Then I have much more to show you," he said as he ordered another. Instead of curry, it just had sprinkled sugar. I wanted to eat it every day of my life.

We spent the next couple of days touring Trivandrum and eating everything in sight. It was so much fun, and I almost wished I could spend all of my time here, but I had work to do. I had come here for a reason, and it was time to start teaching in Kumbalam. I was finally going to see an Indian village.

CHAPTER 3

After two hours on the road, I realized Indian villages were *actual* villages. Back home, small towns were pegged as villages, but were really just called that due to population. In India, villages were tiny places with no cellphone signal, few cars, cute little family owned shops, yards with goats and chickens and stray cows, and almost everyone wore traditional clothes.

It was 5:30 a.m., and Anooj and I were lost. Driving down the road, all we knew was to look for a school with giant pillars called St. Joseph International Academy. Anooj pulled over every time he saw someone to ensure we were on the right path. He said he felt uneasy about this, but I explained Joseph was a family friend. Everything would be fine.

The village was full of short cement fences, like the one at GK's house. Suddenly, a tall curved cement fence with faded orange paint came into view, reading, ENTER WITH AN OPEN MIND. We stopped at the gate, and the guard asked Anooj some questions. I guess the answers satisfied him, because he allowed us to enter.

Just beyond dozens of towering trees, a school with huge blue windows and tall beige pillars loomed in front of me. It looked almost presidential with how grand it was, even more so than the photos. It didn't look real. I noticed a giant soccer field, a second seemingly vacant building, a basketball court, several more trees, and a hostel. I pondered how huge this school was and how lucky this village was to have such a great resource, but about twenty kids stampeded to the car before I could finish my thoughts.

Anooj said something to them in Malayalam, and they laughed. Was it about me?

One boy, about twelve years old, stood at the front. "What is your name, miss?"

"Jurnee. What's your name?"

"Myself, Krishna. Jurnee Miss, I will carry for you." He reached for my backpack.

Why did he say *Miss* at the end of my name? Shouldn't it be at the beginning? I let him carry my backpack, Anooj had my suitcase, and we all entered, like a parade.

Joseph waited just inside. I recognized him immediately from the photos. "Jurnee! I am Joseph D. Fernandez. This is Smitha, our school manager. We're so glad you've made it. How was your trip? How is your family?"

"It was good. They're doing well also. You've got a lovely school!"

We chatted about our mutual expectations, and he showed me to my room.

Krishna asked if he could come, since he had my backpack, and Anooj also followed with my suitcase. We climbed two flights of stairs and passed a metal gate, kind of like the metal one in *Titanic* they used to contain the third-class passengers. The room was small but just as the picture had showed—a double bed, a desk, and a private bathroom.

"Settle in, and come down when you're ready. Tea and breakfast will be ready shortly. The children are just studying before school starts." Joseph handed me an old-fashioned padlock with a giant key. He called Krishna to follow him as he turned to go downstairs.

"Yes, MD Sir."

MD? Like, doctor? I faced Anooj, who immediately noticed my confusion.

"Managing director."

Oh. This will be hard.

Anooj approached the door. "I'll go?"

"Sure. I need to unpack and get ready anyway. Big day!" Of course, I was ready, but I wanted to have my notebook and pen, so I could just go to school and not have to come back up.

"Listen, Jurnee. If you feel at all unsafe or need anything, even just water or a chocolate, call me at any time. I will immediately come."

"Thank you," I said, smiling. What a relief to have a friend nearby in case any problem arose. "I really appreciate it."

He waved, and I watched him leave my room.

I was completely alone. I didn't know anyone. Well, Joseph and Krishna. My heart beat faster. *Not today, anxiety.* Sitting on the bed, I tried to control my breaths as I unpacked my books. I stacked them on the desk and put my makeup and facewash in the bathroom. With a quick glance at my phone, I realized it was getting late.

I stood and walked to the door. Turning around, I surveyed the room and tried to take it all in. This was my home for the next ten weeks. Either this would be the best decision I'd ever made or the worst one. I reminded myself that life was what you make of it and locked the door before heading downstairs, notebook and pen in hand.

A younger girl—maybe eight years old—was sitting and waiting for me halfway down the stairs. She stood when she saw me. "Jurnee Miss! I am waiting so much time. You must come fastly." She took my hand and ran down the stairs to the main area I had just come from, then we turned left into a study hall room.

The rather large room had a few square pillars in the center and a giant picture of Jesus hanging the wall. A small desk held a phone, and a door to the left led into the kitchen. Eight plastic tables, each with four plastic chairs, sat toward the back.

Everyone stared at me, so I gave a nervous wave to the room. Her table had three other girls—two older and another who looked only slightly older.

The girl who had led me down began introductions. "I am Devu, and I am in second standard." She pointed to herself.

I wondered if that meant second grade.

"This is Janaki, and she is in fourth standard." She pointed to the slightly older girl.

Janaki beamed and said hi.

Janaki's sister Radhika was in eighth standard, and Sindhu was in ninth.

I suddenly felt unprepared and wished I had researched more about India's educational system.

Devu and Janaki took turns asking me questions as the older two continued studying. They inquired about my favorite color, favorite food, where I was from, if I'd visited San Francisco, if I was married, my age, and on and on. I loved how curious they were, and their English was much better than I had anticipated. At one point, they compared my hair to golden noodles, probably my favorite thing anyone had ever said.

"Do you have any questions for us?" Janaki asked.

"Actually, yes. How do you keep your hair so nice?" Not one had frizzy hair, even in the bottom tips of their braids. I was amazed.

Sindhu laughed. "Jurnee Miss, just put coconut oil in your hair after bathing."

I noted the pronunciation of *baathing* rather than *baething* and wondered if that was normal. At least it was a simple solution.

An older woman with long wet hair wrapped into a bun with a thin towel came from the kitchen. She said something in Malayalam, and suddenly the boys stood excitedly and followed her into the kitchen.

I looked at Devu in confusion, but Janaki jumped to resolve it. "Jurnee Miss, now is the time for morning tea. After the boys take theirs and return to study hall, then we will take ours."

I wondered why the boys had their tea first, but I doubted a fourth grader was the best person to raise my concerns to, so I let the thought pass.

"You really don't need to be formal. Just *Jurnee* is fine."

"Okay, Jurnee Miss," they reply.

Finally, it was our turn, so we entered the kitchen. Everyone had a small metal cup.

I panicked for a second until the woman, who I presumed to be the cook, pulled an extra cup from behind the pot and smiled at me. She poured mine first and placed it directly into my hand.

"Thank you," I said to her.

She smiled at me again then poured for the girls.

We walked together back to the table to see Joseph standing in the doorway of the study hall. "Students, as you have noticed, we have a guest. This is Jurnee Miss from America. Her hometown is Chicago, the same as President Obama."

This created a bit of a stir; maybe they thought I know him.

"Quiet, quiet, quiet. She will be with us until the end of the term, so please make her feel welcomed. Do not give her any problems. She has the same authority as your other teachers."

They settled down, and he walked to our table. "The daily timetables are posted near the front door. Please review them when you're able and remember them." He spoke sternly but kindly.

The kids seemed to really respect him.

Devu took my cup with hers into the kitchen. I would have taken it myself had I known she was going there, but I let it slide. She returned a moment later and announced it was time for gardening.

Gardening? I hadn't noticed any gardens when I arrived this morning. Sure, there were lots of trees, but I didn't see any flowers or vegetable beds.

She grabbed my hand and led me from the study hall room.

Janaki took my other hand, and, as soon as we reached the staircase, almost in unison, they told me to wait.

I watched them run up the stairs then survey the entry room. I spotted the schedule on the wall.

Hostel Timetable
Monday – Friday

5:00 – 5:10   Wake Up And Abulations

5:10 – 5:20   Prayers

5:20 – 5:50   Exercise, Jogging, Yoga

5:50 – 5:55   Prepare For Class With Books, Assignment Books, Diary

5:55 – 6:45   English Grammar Or General Knowledge

6:45 – 6:55   Tea. Boys First, Girls Once Boys Have Sat Down

6:55 – 7:55   Gardening

7:45 – 8:20   Bath In Two Groups

8:20 – 8:30   School Preparations

8:30 – 8:50   Breakfast. Boys First, Then Girls

9:00 – 12:20   In School

12:20 – 12:50   Lunch Time. Boys First, Girls Once Boys Have Sat Down

12:50 – 4:00   In School

4:30 – 5:30   Sports

5:30 – 6:00   Bath

6:00 – 8:00   Study, Tuition

8:00 – 8:15   Prayer

8:15 – 8:35   Dinner. Boys First, Girls Once Boys Have Sat Down

8:35 – 9:00   Diary Writing And Books In Bag

9:00   Brushing, Prayer, Bedtime For Students Up To 5th Standard

9:15   Brushing, Prayer, Bedtime For Students 6th – 8th Standard

10:00   Brushing, Prayer, Bedtime For Students 9th – 10th Standard

It seemed so strict, but it must be effective in managing so many kids. The only part that truly perplexed me was girls couldn't get food and tea until the boys have gotten theirs and have sat down. Why was that?

Janaki and Devu ran down the stairs, giggling, with giant buckets.

I snapped a quick picture of the schedule to try to memorize it later then followed them outside. Stepping outside for the first time in proper light, I was amazed by how beautiful it looked and how fresh the air smelled. It was completely different from the bustling city of Trivandrum. Immediately ahead was a cobblestone basketball court. To either side grew short flowering trees. A few dog kennels sat to the right. Giant trees towered everywhere. I wished I knew what they were. I hadn't seen trees like this in real life before, and there were so many of them. It was heaven.

Instead of walking straight out to see the rest of the grounds, we took an immediate right. At first, I thought maybe we'd play with the dogs, but we headed to the waterspout just beside them.

Devu filled her bucket then Janaki's as they softly spoke in Malayalam.

I tried not to be bothered and rather focus on taking in all the sights. I thought I saw bananas growing upside down on one of the trees near the buses. Incredible.

"Jurnee Miss!" I heard a call from behind me. Devu and Janaki struggled to carry the buckets, so I relieved them of their duties.

They proved heavier than I had thought, and even I struggled to carry them.

Across the basketball court, up the stairs, and over the gravel trail, we watered the trees. I learned this entire row was banana trees and just beside were mango and coconut trees, answering my palm tree question.

The other students performed various chores. A few older boys cleaned Joseph's car. The younger boys collected litter. Middle-school-aged boys used tools to dig moat-like structures around the base of the banana trees. They took water to fill the moats before putting leaves and other debris on top of the moats. Apparently, this was to help them retain the large amounts of water required to bear fruit. I loved that the trees had purpose. At home, it seemed they were all for show. These ones all had actual purpose and were there to feed people. It was unlike anything I'd ever seen.

With Devu's bucket empty, she returned to the spout to fill it.

Janaki dug through the grass and found a peculiar-looking brown leaf that appeared quite brittle. She licked it and placed it on my head.

I laughed nervously and continued helping her pour the water onto the base of the trees.

"Jurnee Miss, why laughing? It didn't yet happen."

"What didn't happen?" I had no idea what to expect, and I began to reach for my head when I suddenly heard a clicking sound.

The brittle pod exploded, and the seed shot in Janaki's direction. She cried with laughter, and I can't help but to join her. What a fun plant. This place felt so alive. I asked the name but didn't understand their response. Back home, the only fun plant I could think of were the helicopter seeds that float down in a glided rotation when dropped.

Suddenly, a man approached. "What are you doing, Janaki?"

"Secret." She giggled.

"Cigarette, *aa*?" he said with a panic, regarding me like I was corrupting the children.

"No Rizwan Sir. *Seeeecret.*"

"You must be Jurnee Miss," he said with a relieved smile. "I am Muhammed Rizwan, but everyone calls me Rizwan Sir."

"Nice to meet you."

"They say you are from America."

"Yes."

"San Francisco?"

"No, Chicago. It's in the northern central region."

"Nice place."

I smiled and nodded in agreement but couldn't understand the fascination with San Francisco.

Just then, my phone buzzed. Anooj. *Hi, Jurnee. I just reached my home. Is everything ok there? Let me know if you feel any danger or need anything. I can come anytime.*

I smiled. *Everything is ok here, thank you.* Back home I may have found it odd, but I was slowly learning that people here were just much more hospitable than back at home.

"Okay," Rizwan said as he walked away. "Carry on. Let me know if you need anything. Don't let the children become too rowdy."

Everyone was looking at me, but no one was speaking to me. Maybe they were too shy to talk to strangers or foreigners, or to speak English.

Janaki continued watering the trees, and Devu returned with a fresh bucket of water.

I watched them work and noticed all the students were working diligently to maintain the property.

A small boy approached me. "Jurnee Miss?"

"Yes. And what is your name?"

"Solomon." He pronounced it *so-low-moan*, with long *O* sounds rather than *saw-luh-min*, as we would back home. He couldn't be more than six years old. I wondered where his parents were. "Jurnee Miss, time."

I checked my phone and saw it was 7:50. Cross referencing this with the photo I had taken of the schedule, I realized gardening time had reached the end.

He ran inside excitedly, and the others regarded me to find the source of the commotion.

"Seven fifty," I said.

They eagerly carried their tools and buckets inside. The boys walked down the left hallway while the girls went upstairs. I followed, still carrying my notebook all this time, and laid on the bed. *Can I do this?*—answering simple questions, being stared at. I felt completely out of place. Would I make my own place here? Would I ever fit in? I felt like a zoo animal.

With a sigh, I rolled over and copied the schedule from the photo into my notebook. At least it would allow me to clear my mind for a few minutes.

I heard a loud knock from the bottom half of the door. Definitely a child. Opening the door, I saw Solomon from earlier had come upstairs. He looked up at me with the biggest brown eyes and chubby cheeks. "Miss. Biscuit."

I remembered from Anooj's crash course in Indian English that biscuits were cookies. With a welcoming nod, I invited him inside, and he followed. Breakfast was in just a few minutes, but it wouldn't hurt to make a new friend. I pulled a small packet of Dark Fantasy cookies from my bag. They were delicious buttery wafers with a fudgy chocolate filling sandwiched in the middle.

Upon seeing it, the sides of his mouth turned up into a mischievous grin. He quickly snatched them and ran downstairs.

Of course, friendships with small children who don't know English were entirely contingent on your present stock of snacks.

As he left, Sindhu entered, holding a blue plastic bottle. "Jurnee Miss, use this coconut oil." She poured some into her hand, rubbed her palms together and beckoned me by nodding her face downward. "Always use this after head bath. It will make your hair stronger also." She massaged the tiny pea-sized amount into my scalp and down the lengths of my waist-length hair. She beamed with approval as she left it on the table and approached the door. "I'll just go and come."

It was getting late, but I sat and waited for her to return. She must have just gone to get something quickly and would be back in a minute. But, after about fifteen minutes, I realized she wasn't coming back.

I figured it was past time to go downstairs for breakfast, so I gathered my things. Shoes, check. Notebook, check. Pen, check. Phone, check. Padlock, check. I clutched everything and backed out of the room, closing the giant padlock. It felt like I was in another dimension, but this could really be the start of an amazing adventure. I slipped the key into my pocket with my phone and pen and finally went downstairs.

I walked through the main area, down the corridor, and into the study hall room as I noticed a couple kids walking through the side door. I followed them, full of hope. My hope was equally split between food being beyond the doorway and that I'd like the food. I didn't have any reason to think that I wouldn't, it was just nerves. As I entered, I noticed a giant metal bowl full of *idli*, which I was now relatively familiar with. It was a thick white cake about the size of a fist. It didn't have a lot of flavor on its own, but it paired well with chutneys and curries. Another metal bowl contained some sort of chickpea mixture in a brown gravy.

She started to give me four *idli*, and I meekly raised two fingers, indicating I could no way consume all four of them. She looked slightly offended, but compromised and gave three. I thanked her as she poured my chickpea mixture onto the plate.

Then it suddenly occurred to me. How would I eat? I couldn't eat this with my hands. I was still scarred from my failed *dosa* experiment. I had begun to return to study hall but turned around, and she eyed me as though asking, *What happened?*

"I need a spoon."

She seemed confused, and I felt awful for assuming she knew English.

"Spoon," I said slowly as I made a scooping motion in the direction of the food.

The kids giggled, and I felt my face reddening. *Great impression you're making there, Jurnee. Diva foreigner, can't eat without a spoon.* I smiled at them as she brought me a spoon. As I thanked her again, one of the boys asked why I say *thank you* so much. Was that not normal here?

"Jurnee Miss, sit with us," a lisped voice from behind me commanded. A young boy walked around in front of me to direct me to his table. "I am Vishnu."

"Good morning, Vishnu. What grade are you in?"

"My marks are good."

Ohh. They said *standard* here, not *grade*. "Great! Which standard?"

"Fifth standard, ma'am. My brother is in tenth. He is Vivek. This year, he has exams."

"Best of luck to him."

"What did you get on your tenth exams?"

What was a tenth exam? Was that like the ACTs? "Twenty-seven," I replied as a small crowd formed around us.

"How did you get so less of a score?"

"It's on a thirty-six scale."

Everyone just sat around us eating and listening, no one said a word apart from Vishnu and me.

"But it is less, na. You should have studied more. What is your job?"

"I don't have a job yet, still searching." This was worse than a Thanksgiving interrogation. Wow. Now a bunch of kids could judge me for my employment failures too. Great.

"What did you study?"

"I graduated in early childhood education."

"Means teaching?"

"Yes."

He grunted and then ate.

I followed suit. It was delicious, and I wanted to eat this all day, every day. "Vishnu?"

"Yes, Miss?"

"What is this called?"

He said something I couldn't quite decipher.

"What is it?"

Again, I had absolutely no idea what he'd said and admitted defeat by thanking him.

"Always telling thank you. Don't be so serious."

"Sorry."

"Jurnee Miss, friends don't tell sorry or thank you. ~ool."

A fifth grader had just told me, in front of a bunch of other kids, that I wasn't cool. I laughed to myself as I continued eating my breakfast. At least he considered us friends though; I'd made some progress. Hopefully, everyone else here was as friendly, and they were just shy right now.

I saw Joseph entering from the hall, and he quickly approached our table. "Are you ready?"

"Yes."

"Okay. When you finish, I'll be in my office. The rest of you, finish eating quickly. Don't disturb her so much."

I nodded and took my last couple of bites as he walked away. Suddenly, a wave of anxiety hit me. Where was his office? Was I supposed to know? I looked at Vishnu, and he gave me a confused look. "Vishnu?"

"Yes, miss?"

"Where is his office?"

"We will show you. Finish your food."

A guided tour, how exciting. I always worried for nothing. Everything would be fine.

As soon as I finished eating, one of the boys brought my plate and spoon into the kitchen and another took my notebook. The boy with the notebook and Vishnu stood together and beckoned me to join them. The office ended up being just down the hallway, second door on the right.

I thanked them but was met with protests. "Enough, Jurnee Miss. Stop this *thank you, thank you*."

No one had ever scolded me to *stop* using manners, and I chortled. "Okay, fine." I smiled and nodded.

"Make sure to come to my class, fifth standard. Don't forget."

"No! Mine! Third standard!"

"I'll try, but I don't know where they'll send me." As I turned to knock, I hoped I would end up with familiar faces. Introductions could get exhausting, but so far, they'd been pretty successf—

My thoughts stopped abruptly as I realized the door had been open this entire time, and he could hear us talking. I felt my face redden, and I looked down in embarrassment. Nothing was embarrassing, but I couldn't help the feeling.

"Ready?" Joseph asked as he closed the book he was reading.

As soon as I said *yes*, he stood and took his padlock and bag. He locked the door, and we walked together through the foyer and out the front door, across the basketball court and passed the dog cages, up the few stairs and then to his car at the right—a white Hyundai, shiny from the cleaning this morning. The school sat just across the way though, why drive? I didn't want to question him too much, as I was a guest here, so I followed and approached the front door on the right side.

"You want to drive?" he asked.

I had completely forgotten the cars were right-hand drivers. Good job, Jurnee. I quickly walked to the passenger side and slid in. As I fastened my seatbelt, he pulled the car forward toward the wall.

He noticed my panic and chuckled. "There's a superstition here. It's bad luck to start a car going backwards. It is a parallel into our lives that we should always move forward."

What a nice sentiment—a bit odd and potentially dangerous, but overall nice. We reversed and drove about a hundred yards to the next building, where we went up the front stairs into the school's main office.

A woman in her early thirties sat at the desk and beamed as I approached. "You must be Jurnee Miss! Welcome to our school!" she exclaimed with a hug.

I loved it here.

Another woman passed the corner.

"Jurnee, this is Nissy Miss. She is our principal."

She was beautiful. I smiled and said a nearly silent hello.

"Welcome, dear. Please come and sit." She led me into her office. She seemed so kind and open, like an older sister.

"Now, tell me. What is the secret to your beauty?"

I will never leave. I officially loved India more than any place that had ever existed. Everyone had been so nice to me.

I gave a sheepish smile and looked down; I didn't know how to answer and now I was completely embarrassed.

"You are from America?"

"Yes, ma'am. Chicago."

"And you studied teaching?"

"Yes, ma'am." I smiled at the irony; I was finally at my first teaching interview.

"Okay, dear. Here are some cards that will help with the younger students for alphabets. If you need any materials or help, just come here, and I'll try to get anything that you need." She handed me a pile of alphabet flash cards.

A loud boom comes from the other side of the wall.

"The assembly is beginning," Nissy Miss said.

"What?" I couldn't hear anything over the banging.

"Assembly! Come!"

My first day as an actual teacher was now beginning. This was what everything had come down to. Despite how nervous and frantic my internal monologue was, I felt strangely calm. This was what I had wanted for the past ten years and desperately needed for the past six months. It was finally time.

CHAPTER 4

She took my hand and walked me to a stage, looking over all the standing children in rows. I saw what I assumed to be the school band's percussion section, just a handful of students at the front of the courtyard with their deafening drums. As I looked across the audience, the students' mouths dropped in surprise. A few poked each other to look, a few beamed smiles, but most stared, just like in Trivandrum.

As Joseph approached the microphone, the banging stopped. He addressed everyone to welcome them back from Christmas break before Nissy Miss said a few words, followed by my introduction. She waved me over to speak. Me? Speak? I couldn't possibly.

I stepped forward and scanned the assembly. There weren't many student, just a few hundred, but it may as well have been thousands. I gulped and smiled before speaking into the microphone. "Hello, everyone. My name is Jurnee, and I'm from America. I've come to visit and teach for the next few weeks. I studied teaching and can't wait to get to know all of you." I hoped that was sufficient as I looked to Nissy Miss for silent approval.

She smiled at me, and I was washed with relief.

She continued speaking but changed to Malayalam, and I stood still, as not to distract anyone from what she was saying.

After a few minutes, some students approached the stage and participated in some guided exercises.

I looked around and luckily none of the other teachers were doing them, only the students, so I didn't have to make a fool of myself quite yet.

The students left the stage, and everyone stood to attention with their hand on the shoulder of the person in front of them, arm outstretched. In unison, they began, *"India is my country. All Indians are my brothers and sisters. I love my country, and I am proud of its rich and varied heritage. I shall always strive to be worthy of it. I shall give my parents, teachers, and all elders respect and treat everyone with courtesy. To my country and my people, I pledge my devotion. In their wellbeing and prosperity, alone lies my happiness."*

Their pledge was so heartwarming. I loved the personal touches to it compared with the American one. *All Indians are my brothers and sisters … I shall give my parents, teachers, and all elders respect.* Nothing like that is in ours. It had such a sweet sentiment.

Suddenly, the banging of the drums began again, and I looked to Nissy Miss for direction on what to do.

"Jurnee Miss. Go to Lovely Miss's LKG classroom exactly across the courtyard. Come after one hour, and we will have drafted a schedule for you."

I wasn't sure what LKG was, but it definitely wasn't any of the grade levels the kids in the hostel had mentioned during breakfast. With my notebook and alphabet letters,

I set off for the LKG classroom. A short walk across the courtyard brought me to a door with a small plaque labelled, LKG.

With a knock on the door, I peeked my head inside. "Lovely Miss?" I hadn't heard *Lovely* as a name before. It was so cute and unique.

"Oh! Jurnee Miss! Welcome to our Kerala. Have you eaten?"

I nodded. "We had *idli* in the hostel."

"Good, good." She gave an approving smile and sat at the desk in front of the room. It seemed a bit dingy compared to normal classrooms back home, but it contained all of the usual items—educational posters, desks, chairs, games, books. "Class, sit! It is time for roll call."

"Yes, Lovely Miss," they said in unison as they sat in their tiny chairs.

I tried to figure out what LKG meant but was unsuccessful.

She called name by name, and they confirmed their presence, same as any school. As soon as she finished, she faced me and said, "I'll go and come," leaving me alone with twenty small kids who barely knew English.

I chuckled nervously. Maybe she went to get some water or to use the restroom or to ask Nissy Miss something. After a few minutes, I began to wonder if I had misunderstood and I was actually their sole teacher for the next hour.

"Get ahold of yourself, Jurnee," I muttered to force myself back into reality. "Okay, class! My name is Jurnee Miss, and I am from America." I spoke slowly and tried to enunciate every syllable, just in case they understood something.

"Ameerika?" a few of them exclaimed then chattered amongst themselves.

"Yes, yes. And today, we will study the alphabet."

I heard the familiar moan of kids not wanting to study. I guess some things transcend languages and borders.

I opened the alphabet cards and showed the letter *A*. "What letter is this?"

"*A* for apple!"

If they already knew English, then why was I here? "Wow, great!" I took the next.

"*B* for boy!"

Had they studied all of the letters?

"*C* for cat!"

Okay, I'll just go a little further into the cards to see where they have left off.

"*L* for lion!"

Okay, let's go further.

"*S* for snake!"

I didn't know what to do after the cards ran out, and they seemingly fed off my uncertainty, beginning again the chatter amongst themselves. I flipped the last card with a shred of hope I could teach them something.

"*Zed* for zebra!"

At first, I was confused, but then I remembered reading Indian English is primarily derived from British English. I scanned the room. What could I teach them next?

The chattering grew, and I was terrified of seeming incapable. I felt like giving up and asking for help, but then I saw a nursey rhyme on the wall. Or rather, what I assumed to be a nursey rhyme. It was something about a boy called Johnny.

Johnny, Johnny.
Yes, Papa?
Eating sugar?
No, Papa.
Telling lies?
No, Papa.
Open your mouth.
Ha ha ha!

I tried to recall any rhyme and felt the lightbulb in my head immediately turn on.

"Today, we will learn a new nursey rhyme."

The chatter changed from scattered to very centralized and *very* excited.

I really wanted to know how much English they comprehended so I knew what I could communicate with them, but I wasn't sure how to ask. I stood at the center of the front of the room and waved my hands to invite them to stand also.

They seemed very excited to stop sitting.

"I'm a little teapot," I started, speaking loudly and clearly.

They eyed me, confused.

"You also say. 'I'm. A. Little. Tea. Pot.'"

Uncertain voices spoke the words softly and nervously.

"I'm. A. Little. Tea. Pot." I smiled and waved my hands for them to try again to join me.

"I'm a little tea *pot*." They got it right, but I wasn't sure why they had put such an emphasis on *pot*.

"Short. And. Stout."

The uncertain and scattered voices tried again.

Maybe if I showed them the full form of the rhyme with the actions, they'd be more motivated. "Watch, and then we'll try."

With eyes wide, they waited for the show.

"I'm a little teapot, short and stout." I acted the motions of squatting to emphasize *short* and put my hands at my waist to emphasize *stout*. "Here is my handle." I put my left hand on my hip to mimic a handle. "And here is my spout." I outstretched my right hand, palm up, to create the spout.

They were mesmerized.

"When I get all steamed up, hear me shout." In a slightly higher decibel, I finished, "*Tip me over, and pour me out!*" I leaned as far as I could toward my arm-spout to mimic pouring tea.

They were amazed.

I saw every eye awestruck by my magnificent performance. Just when I thought everything would be fine, I noticed none other than Nissy Miss and Lovely Miss stood at the door, and my face immediately reddened. What if they had hated it and thought I was turning the children into hooligans?

"Jurnee Miss! Wonderful! You must teach us more of these rhymes from America!"

Lovely Miss relieved me of my duties, and I followed Nissy Miss to her office. As we walked through the courtyard, every student peaked at us through the windows.

Nissy Miss asked me to notate more rhymes, so they could incorporate them into their future curriculum. I jotted it down in my notebook quickly before I forgot.

When we reached her office, Nissy Miss handed me the schedule she and the secretary had drafted for me. It seemed that today I would be visiting UKG, I, and II. I and II could be inferred to be first and second grade, but what on earth was this LKG and UKG?

"Nissy Miss?"

"Yes, *mollu*?"

I'll ask Anooj what that means later.

"What are LKG and UKG? We don't have them in America."

"Well, of course you do. It is lower kindergarten and upper kindergarten, the ages before formal school."

Oh. So, it was basically pre-k and kindergarten. That made so much more sense. "Thank you!"

"No need for telling thank you," she kindly scolded me.

I really needed to learn to be less polite.

I took the schedule in my notebook and left in search of the UKG classroom but immediately stopped.

Janaki from the hostel stood in the courtyard with a teacher.

"You are the Jurnee Miss, correct?"

"Yes, ma'am." I was suddenly struck by the irony that I needed to be less formal with manners but more formal with titles to fit in around here.

"You have met Janaki? From hostel? You know she is half Russian."

"Wow, really?" That was actually pretty cool. I didn't know any other foreigners lived around here.

"Yes. That is why she is so beautiful and fair. Like you."

I felt my smile fade. This wasn't the first time I had heard this association with fairness and beauty. Why did people here associate skin color so closely with how attractive someone was? I suppose some did it in the US to some extent but not this vocally.

"No, ma'am. Fair and dark are equally beautiful."

She was a bit taken aback by my statement, and they continued walking.

I hoped I hadn't made her angry or had offended in any way, I just wished people realized skin color only relied on the amount of melanin provided based on the evolutionary and biological need of someone's ancestral region. People with more melanin actually had many more health benefits. Maybe I could say something in an assembly. Or would that be weird? I hushed my thoughts when I realized I had been standing still in the middle of the courtyard with my thoughts like a weirdo.

I quickly resumed my search for the UKG classroom and circled the courtyard. The rooms seemed to be in order of grade level, and it was soon apparent the UKG classroom was just to the right of the LKG classroom, and I had just wasted a ton of time trying to find it and surely looking foolish in the process.

I entered the room to see a lady sitting up front at a desk.

She pointed to herself and said, "Meenakshi Miss." Her daughter was apparently in this class also, and they looked exactly alike. After a moment, it seemed she would stay with me, but she also said, "I'll go and come," before leaving indefinitely.

Was I missing something?

I stood at the front of the class and introduced myself again. "Good morning. I am Jurnee Miss. What are your names?"

Suddenly, they shouted in unison, "*Good morning, miss.*"

It was a bit off-putting at first but charming.

They then took turns going around the room to introduce themselves. The names ranged from incredibly long to super short. I heard a Prathabalakshmikanthan but also a Peter. I wondered if a reason existed between such vastly different names.

I asked them what they were studying, and I saw a wave of confusion wash across their faces. Of course, they were just kids and didn't have good English skills yet. I quickly scanned the room for hints. Posters hung on the walls of colors and body parts. Maybe that was a good starting point.

As we reviewed all of the colors and body parts, they seemed bored. Maybe we could try rhymes in this class as well. "Watch this, and then we will do together."

Their tired faces immediately perked up.

With the motions, I began, "Head and shoulders, knees and toes. Knees and toes. Head and shoulders, knees and toes. Knees and toes. And eyes and ears and mouth and nose. Head and shoulders, knees and toes. Knees and toes."

They were transfixed, just as the LKG students had been.

"Do you want to try now?"

Cheers erupted, and I nervously looked out the window. I really didn't like having open windows in every classroom. It was great for accountability in that anyone could see everything at any time, but I felt like they already stared at me so much that it just made me feel very uneasy. Luckily, the other classes must have been busy, and no one came to complain about the sudden eruption of sound.

We started to sing "Head and Shoulders" together, with motions, when I remembered something from my childhood. We used to try to go faster and faster to see who could do it the best. "Let's try again but faster."

They looked side to side, giggling to each other.

I was doing it. I was teaching.

We began again, but this time faster. And then again just a little faster. And again even faster. The giggles and squeals continued throughout, and I couldn't believe they actually liked me. I was teaching them; we were playing. We could barely communicate, but they were learning and having fun.

We continued playing with various rhymes, changing it up after every few rounds to keep them engaged, but they really seemed to enjoy it.

The bell rang, and I checked my schedule. Onto first grade. Or no, first *standard*. That'll take some getting used to.

I remembered the classrooms were in order and walked just next door to the next room. I began the same way. "Good morning. I am Jurnee Miss. What are your names?"

Again, they shouted in unison, "*Good morning, miss!*" They were quite a bit louder than the UKG group though. It was almost as if they were having a competition of who could shout it the loudest, and the prize was my burst eardrums.

The teacher smiled and left the room. Maybe I was the relief teacher for their planning period.

"What are you studying right now?" I asked them, hopeful we might do something more challenging. As expected, a wave of confusion washed over them.

One girl confidently stood at her seat. "Jurnee Miss, we are right now learning multiplication." They were way ahead of American schools.

We ended up using the class period to discuss their curriculum. Her English was phenomenal, and they already knew multiplication and cursive. She took her notebook and a pen and asked for my autograph. Reluctantly, I agreed to sign despite being a no one.

Suddenly, the whole class stood and walked to the front, asking for my autograph. They kept pushing harder and harder, and I was amazed by the strength of this first grade mob as I tried to sign every notebook. Within moments, I was buried in children.

Luckily the bell rang, and the students flooded into the courtyard.

I breathed a sigh of exhausted relief as I relished in this empty classroom. During my time student teaching, I had never felt as tired as I felt right now. Was it because the language barrier was more mentally tiring or because I was solely responsible for a class with whom I could barely communicate? I wasn't sure, but a thousand thoughts swirled in my mind about how I could improve the classes tomorrow. I could research more rhymes, we could sing songs, improve their vocabulary so we could communicate more effectively. I took note of these, and that Joseph wanted me to practice their accents with them, in my notebook.

I saw some of the hostel students near the front of the courtyard and walked toward them.

"Good afternoon, Jurnee Miss."

"Good afternoon, Devu Miss. Good afternoon, Janaki Miss."

They giggled at my strangely formal greeting, but it was fun to tease them. I didn't want everyone to be formal with me, since I wasn't here for a long time. I wanted them to see me as their friend so we could really dig deep into their confidence in speaking. By removing that formality, they hopefully wouldn't feel as much hesitation in speaking with me.

"Want to see something cool?" I asked.

They looked curiously to one another before simultaneously agreeing.

"This is something we did when I was in school in America."

Their eyes illuminated.

"Put your hands like this," I instructed them with my right hand facing the ground and my left hand facing the ceiling. I moved my hands to meet Janaki's and, after they clapped, moved my right hand to face the ceiling and my left hand to face the ground. I then moved my palms slowly to her to indicate they should meet perpendicularly to the floor, and finally clapped on my own and began again.

It worked. Delight bloomed in their eyes as other students spied and imitated us. But we were soon interrupted.

"Come, miss. It is time for lunch. We will go back to the hostel."

It suddenly dawned on me; there wasn't a cafeteria—no microwaves or refrigerators. I saw children eating from round metal boxes. Did everyone bring food from home? There was no hot lunch? I asked Janaki and Devu about it, and they confirmed as we walked to the hostel.

As we reached the front door, we saw some other students from the hostel already gathered. They were knocking on the door, calling for someone inside to let them in.

When I approached, they turned and smiled. "Good afternoon, Jurnee Miss."

"Good Afternoon, Vivek Sir. Good Afternoon, Sajith Sir."

They also looked confused and then laughed. Hopefully, they were laughing with me and not at me.

Vivek's younger brother, Vishnu, said something in Malayalam, and Vivek walked to the side of the building by the sinks. Soon we saw him through the windows approaching the front door to let us in. He said something to the other students, and we all went inside.

I suddenly felt alone, despite being surrounded by others. It was one thing when the students couldn't understand me, but it was another thing entirely to be surrounded by people who could understand me without me knowing what was happening. They could have at least told me what was going on. Why were they keeping a secret?

It's not a secret. They aren't used to your presence, the sane part of my mind finally piped up as we made our way to the kitchen. *If it was important, they would have told you. You can't expect them to completely change how they communicate just because you're here. Don't be selfish.*

My mind constantly battled between thinking the worst and thinking logically. Everyone was really sweet; I was sure they didn't intend to make me feel excluded. I made a mental note to be less hesitant with everyone as we entered the kitchen. This was a fresh start with new people, but despite this revelation, I'd been wasting time I could have been interacting with my new housemates.

"Jurnee Miss." A voice from behind woke me from my thoughts. "Cook Auntie is waiting for you."

I had completely forgotten we were standing in line to eat. I held my plate closer to the bowl as he scooped rice and two curries onto my plate. I thanked him and he smiled, but now came the difficult part—where should I sit?

Returning to the study hall room, I realized the problems from my school days would be the least of my problems now. Hands at every table beckoned me to join them. The hopeful glimmer in their eyes quickly faded as I sat at the girls table.

"Jurnee Miss. Tell us about America," they asked almost in unison.

"Actually, first, I have one small question."

"What is it?"

"Why is the rice so big?" I'd eaten rice before many times, but it had always been thin and somewhat long. It always looked the same, but the rice here was totally different. It was short and quite fat, maybe three times the circumference of normal rice. Would it taste the same?

The girls looked confused. "The rice is normal size only. What do you mean?"

"In America, our rice is long and thin. I haven't seen thick rice like this before."

"You only eat *biriyani*?"

"No. It's just different at home."

Devu sweetly looked up from her plate. "Jurnee Miss, this is your home now."

I smiled at her, and we finished our lunch as the girls chatted in Malayalam.

After lunch, Nissy Miss instructed me to wait in the office for her. I decided to strike up a conversation to get to know the secretary. "Good Afternoon, Ajitha Miss. How's it going?"

She looked confused. "I'm not going anywhere. It is school time only."

I was confused for a moment then remembered how it sounded in literal terms to ask how it was going. I made a mental note to only ask how people were in the future.

Andriya, one of the older students, walked into the office. I had met her earlier while speaking with her younger brother Winston in the hall.

"How are you?" I asked her.

"I am fine. How are you?"

"I am also fine."

Nissy Miss came, and Andriya followed her into her office.

I thumbed through the photo albums on the table while I waited. They were full of photos with students in really cute matching clothes with a heading of Annual Day. I had never heard of Annual Day before. A day that happens annually? What was the big deal?

Andriya emerged from Nissy Miss's office and waved to me as she returned to class.

"Jurnee Miss!" Nissy Miss called me to her office, extending her arm with the palm spread and patting her hand downward.

I had seen a few people calling people like this, but back home, we generally put our palm upward and only move the fingers, not the whole hand. I had seen it in Trivandrum but hadn't given it a second thought. Maybe that was just how people here did things.

We entered her office. "Jurnee, dear, MD Sir is in Trivandrum on business so could not tell you personally, but we wanted to give you advance notice that there is no class tomorrow. Tomorrow there will be a *bandh*."

A Bundt? Like the cake? "What is that?"

"Here there will sometimes be a *bandh*. It is very complicated, but it is a small political issue, and we want to keep the children safe, so all schools will be closed."

"Just for the day or will it take more time?"

"It should be just the day. Sometimes it will be two. But since it is a Friday, we should be back in session for Monday." She saw my concern. "Don't be alarmed. It's completely normal. Also, please follow Lovely Miss after school to help her with bus duty."

I wasn't entirely sure what that consisted of, but after school, I went to her classroom.

"Jurnee Miss, come," she instructed as I followed her outside to the buses.

We went inside, and I was immediately shocked at how different yet the same buses were. They were yellow. The seats were the same shape, same thickness, and same rough vinyl-covered seats. But a lot more kids were in the bus, and some even sat in the front with the driver.

My role was to help the younger students down the stairs and hand their heavy school bags to their parents. It wasn't hard work; it just required two people—one to sit with the kids while the other walked them down the stairs.

I always loved an opportunity to get out and see the village, but something different stuck me this time. The father of two students picked them up in a boat. A boat! It was a small fishing boat, and they entered it from a small dock before rowing across the backwaters. I looked around and was the only one amazed. This was their normalcy, but it was my paradise. Well, *almost* paradise. There was no Wi-Fi and I rarely had cell phone signal.

The next morning, Joseph was still in Trivandrum, so Rizwan Sir was in charge. He said we were to follow the weekend schedule, so they decided we would wash our clothes. But how? I didn't see any washers or dryers anywhere.

"Rizwan Sir, where is the laundry room?"

"Jurnee Miss, this is not your America. We are not that much spoiled. We will wash with our hands only."

With our hands? I was so confused.

"Nelson-ay! Vishnu-ay! Come and help Jurnee Miss to wash her clothes."

This wasn't the first time I had heard people adding *ay* to names when they shouted. I briefly wondered what it meant, but their presence interrupted my thoughts.

"Yes, sir," they said in unison as they came to my side. They followed behind me, like baby ducks, as we went upstairs to my room to get my clothes.

"Jurnee Miss, do you have a bucket?" Nelson asked.

"There's one in the bathroom."

"Okay, miss," Vishnu said as they stood in the hallway while I went inside. "You want to take any dress that you wish to wash and bring it in that bucket."

Dress? Oh, right. Dress meant any article of clothing. They had amazing English, but our dialects were so different.

While I was in the bathroom getting the bucket, something fell on my head, and I couldn't stifle the scream.

Nelson and Vishnu ran to see if I was okay, but meanwhile, a parade of elephants stampeded upstairs to see what had happened.

A lizard had fallen on my head, and I was mortified.

One by one, they banged on the door to make sure I was okay. "Jurnee Miss, is it paining?"

Paining? I had a brief moment of confusion until I realized they probably meant to ask if I was in pain. I was not injured, but my ego was. Once it was determined I was not critically injured, the concerned stampede traipsed downstairs.

Nelson and Vishnu again asked if I was okay before briefly teasing me. Apparently, lizards were common here, but luckily, they weren't dangerous. They confirmed, laughing, that there was no risk of biting.

On the way out, I grabbed my jeans and shirts, opting to save the underwear to wash in the privacy of my own room. We walked together downstairs and out the front hostel doors and toward the dog cages and waterspout but then continued onward. At the edge of the cement gate that circled the property sat a giant slab of concrete. It wasn't at all rough. It was perfectly smooth, and it came up just a little past my knees. To the right was another waterspout. The slab was just wide enough for the three of us to each spread a shirt.

"Jurnee Miss, first you want to fill your bucket with water," Nelson began.

After I filled my bucket, he continued, "Then you want to make it inside out, so the cotton won't become rough."

We each spread a shirt, and I followed their lead as they poured some water onto it. Vishnu pulled two bars of blue soap from his clothes pile in the bucket. They were like normal soap but with ridges—an ingenious way to make built-in scrubbing for better cleaning.

"I brought an extra for you."

"Thank you so much, Vishnu. I really appreciate it."

Nelson interrupted. "Jurnee Miss, that is my soap."

"Oh sorry. Then thank you, Nelson."

I followed their lead as they scrubbed the shirt with soap. Once we had enough bubbles, we flipped it upside down and scrubbed the soap onto the other side. Then we rubbed the shirt against itself on the slab to remove any dirt or stains. Finally, we rinsed it off with a bit of water and put them at edge of the slab in front of us. It took a lot of time and strength for a single article of clothing, but it wasn't as difficult as I had anticipated. Jeans were another story altogether. Luckily, they had packed an extra scrub brush for me because we had to scrub them very hard to remove all the dirt. Handwashing jeans was not for the fainthearted.

After we had washed the last piece, we wrung out the clothes as much as we could and put all our wet clothes into the bucket. We walked toward the basketball court and, despite having wrung them out for the most part, the buckets were extremely heavy.

"Where will we hang them?"

"Miss, we do not hang them. This is why we wait for weekend, because we lay them on the steps and on the basketball court."

They each pulled one item from their bucket and helped each other wring it out. They didn't simply twist it. They pulled it, pressed it, twisted it more than I had known was even possible. It was practically dry by the time they had finished.

I guess they noticed how intrigued I was, because Vishnu said, "Jurnee Miss, do not worry. We will do this for you. We are stronger than you are."

I was slightly offended until I realized it was probably true and couldn't help but chuckle. "Okay, you win," I admitted my defeat as they wrung out everything and arranged them neatly on the ground for optimum sunlight.

"We will come after a few hours to collect them," the boys informed me.

This was way harder than doing laundry at home.

That evening, I checked my phone for the first time since arriving. I had been much busier than I had anticipated. I scrolled through frantic messages from my parents, some from my friends, lots from Anooj.

I started my replies with my parents. *Sorry. Got busy. All ok, just settling in.* I hit Send before moving onto my friends' replies. I saved Anooj for last, since I knew he would reply right away. His messages were the same as the others—curiosity at first and a gradual change to concern when they never got a reply.

Everything is fine, just busy. I hand washed laundry, a lizard fell on my head, and I ate giant rice. By the way, why do people end names with AY when they call them? And what is with 'I'll go and come'?? They never come back.

Great! Be safe about the lizards though. Some people believe that you have to visit a specific temple to undo the bad luck it causes. But, as long as it didn't fall on your head, you should be fine. We just use the AY to add emphasis when we call someone. It's nothing special. And we don't like to say bye, so we just say we'll be back.

We all spoke the same language, but it was so different. *Ohh. Thanks! But what if it did fall on my head? What does that mean?*

It means you will die soon. He added a devil emoji.

WHAT! Was he serious? This couldn't actually be legitimate.

There's only one way to fix it.

I replied impatiently with …

Come back to Trivandrum.

"Ha-ha," I said as I locked my phone and went downstairs for dinner.

CHAPTER 5

At last it was Friday night again and that meant one thing, our weekly *pappadam*. It was like a cracker but so much better. And when it got a little soft from the curry, it was perfect. We got them every Friday with dinner, and I had grown to really look forward to it. Only a couple of weeks had passed, but I was already in a familiar rhythm.

For dinner, I sat with the fifth and sixth standard boys. We had absolutely nothing in common, but they were so much fun to talk to. They told me about their teachers, their friends, their families. I told them about life in the US.

I looked over to see what sound was coming from the girls table. They were playing the handclap game.

"Jurnee Miss. Why aren't you eating your dinner?"

I hadn't realized I hadn't yet begun to eat. I eyed the rice, curry, and *pappadam* but felt dread. It was delicious. I was just so tired of rice. Every day for lunch and dinner and then every morning was a rice-based menu, like *idli*, or *puttu*, or *dosa*, or *appam*. How did people eat the same thing for every meal?

The boys noticed my dismay. "Jurnee Miss! What happened?"

"Nothing happened. Everything is fine."

"Was someone mean to you? You look sad," Sachin said.

Vishnu was normally quiet, but even he spoke for me. "We will beat them, miss. Don't take tension."

I love them so much. No one had ever offered to beat up someone on my behalf. "No, no. No one did anything."

"Then what happened?" Nelson asked.

All of them sat forward in their seats, ready to hear what awful fate had befallen their new foreign teacher.

"Actually, I'm tired of rice."

"Rice, *aa*? What is wrong in rice?" They were utterly confused about how someone could be tired of their region's staple food.

"Nothing is wrong. It's very nice. It's just a lot. Every meal, we're having it."

They were still confused. "Then, what do you eat?"

"We have waffles, pizza, burgers, pasta—so many different options."

Rizwan Sir overheard our discussion and added, "But those are all *maida* based. It is very bad for you. These dishes are similar, but they use rice instead of *maida*. Kerala food is the healthiest food."

I remembered that *maida* basically meant *all-purpose flour*. I guess when you thought about it, it was true. "You're right," I said with a smile. I just needed to stop being a diva and work on assimilating better.

"So, Americans only eat *maida* and vending machine snacks?" Aravind asked.

There was instant confusion and overlapping questions about what a vending machine was. How did he know about vending machines?

"A vending machine is a giant box that has snacks or juices and sometimes even grocery items. You put money or slide your credit card, select which item you want and then your selection comes out. We don't eat them very often, but most offices and schools have them."

"How does the food come out?"

I had no idea, but Nelson, the prodigy electrician, interjected with his best effort of a description. "There would be a device which holds an object. It should be controlled by a motor which would activate when you make your selection and give payment."

"Wow! Thanks, Nelson," I said, thinking how a sixth-standard boy could better explain a vending machine than me, an avid user of them.

They made a plan to ask Joseph for a vending machine in the hostel. Everyone was excited until one of them brought up the fact that most of them don't have pocket money available.

"One more question, miss," Aravind added. "Why do you eat only with spoons?"

I couldn't help but to laugh. "I don't know. Our parents teach us to eat with spoons from the time we're small kids."

"Try once to eat with hand."

I could feel the entire room turning to look, curious to see if I would accept the challenge. I hadn't realized how odd it was, but, come to think of it, I was the only one not eating with my hands. "Okay, I'll try ... on one condition."

His ears perked up, and each of the boys leaned in to find out what it would take to see me eat with my hands.

"You all have to try to eat with a spoon for one meal."

They giggled amongst themselves, nodded their heads from side to side and turned, in unison, to look at me. "Deal." Without another word, they all went to the kitchen.

I guess this was the moment of truth. Could I eat with my hand? Or would this be another *dosa* disaster?

They emerged with spoons. This was the moment of truth.

"Ready, Jurnee Miss?"

Rizwan Sir had moved to our table to observe.

"Put your fingers down on the plate, mix the rice with your fingers, then make a ball, and use all five fingers to put in your mouth," they explained.

It sounded simple but was a lot more complicated than that. I did as instructed, but it was a disaster. "Why am I so bad at this?" I jokingly asked them. This was even more difficult than eating the *dosa*.

"After some practice, you will be good. Don't worry."

They were so sweet. I tried a few more bites but didn't even remotely improve. "Okay, your turn."

One by one, they grabbed their spoons, unsure how to hold it. A few of them held it in their fist with their thumb facing downward, some with just their thumb and index finger. They looked very uncomfortable. Like me, they also only lasted a few bites before resuming their familiar method. We all laughed.

I teased them, "Not so easy, eh?"

"Okay, fine. You win," Aravind said, hesitantly relinquishing.

"*Dei*," Rizwan interjected. "You all lose. No one wins." He chuckled at our failure.

After dinner, I'd usually check the rooms to ensure no one was fighting or breaking any rules—mostly just to help out Rizwan—but tonight was different.

When I passed a room, a mysterious voice whispered, "*Pssssst*. Jurnee Miss. Come fastly."

I entered the room, and one of them opened a bag to reveal a giant bag of something that appeared to be an Indian Chex Mix. Another had Dark Fantasy cookies hidden. Another had some Lay's. We shut the door and had our mini feast.

"Jurnee Miss," Karthik started, "my parents have a shop in Varkala. I always have a lot of snacks. If you ever are hungry and don't want rice, I will give anything you wish. Don't ever feel sad."

I couldn't believe the kindness. He could only go home once a month to get snacks, and he was willing to share everything with me. With five of us eating, it didn't take long for us to deplete the snacks. I knew I hadn't been the only one to eat them, but I felt awful.

"I'm so sorry, Karthik. I'll go to town and get more."

"No, miss. It is fine. We go home this weekend. Always you are tensed. Be cool. Relax."

Was it common here to tell people to be cool? I nodded and smiled. "I should be going before Rizwan Sir or MD Sir comes. Goodnight."

"Goodnight, miss," they called in unison.

I shut the door behind me and went upstairs to sleep.

Sunday was church. I hadn't gone to church much back home, but here, we all went together. Many students were Hindu and a few Muslim, but we all attended. Maybe it was compulsory, due to being a Catholic school. Boys wore jeans, and the girls dressed up nicely in their skirts and more decorative styles of earrings. I wore jeans and one of my nicer shirts, though I always felt terribly underdressed compared to the other women in their *sarees*. Some were silk, some were sequined, and some had beautiful patterns. I secretly wished I would get to wear one just once.

I finished getting ready first, so I walked to the foyer of the second floor.

Waiting for me was my dear Solomon, our mischievous angel of the hostel. "Miss. Spin," he said as he stuck both of his arms straight into the air. He noticed my confusion, so he took my hands and ran sideways in a circle. "*Titanic*."

I realized he wanted to spin like Jack and Rose had on *Titanic*. Everyone here was obsessed with *Titanic*. I took his hands, and we ran sideways in a circle.

"Miss! Speed!"

I went faster until he was flying and giggling. "Speed! Speed! Speed!"

I would be red and sweaty with messy hair for church, but it was worth it.

I went downstairs for breakfast, and Joseph approached me. "Jurnee, the girls ride in the car with me usually, but I don't know that we have enough space for another passenger. You help Rizwan with the boys and walk to the church. It isn't far. We will leave in a few minutes."

I began to turn quickly up the stairs when suddenly he stopped me. "Jurnee. A few *Indian* minutes. In *American* minutes, it will be about twenty minutes. Take your time."

I smiled and walked slowly upstairs.

Finally, the time came, and we went in lines of three and four as passed the gate. It was beautiful. Each house had an ornate gate. Some had butterflies, some were simple black, and some were golden. Some of the cement fences were painted purple or other colors; some were covered with hundreds of posters. Some of the posters were for movies; others appeared to be political, featuring old men smiling. Larger-sized banners that matched the political posters adorned others, but some banners had pictures of children giving their scores in an exam. Some of the cement fences been painted with STICK NO BILLS, which evidently warded off the people who posted signs. Many houses had dogs just behind their gates. Some were big and loud; surprisingly, many houses had Pomeranians—just tiny, fluffy white dogs living their best lives.

Out of nowhere, two motorcycles slowed down beside us and shouted something in Malayalam.

The hostel boys shouted back, and Rizwan signaled me to stand behind them. Their exchange lasted a few minutes until the motorcycles sped away as suddenly as they had come.

"What happened?" I asked them, voice shaking.

"Everything is fine. We will always protect you, miss."

They rearranged me to be in the exact middle before we began again to church. For some reason, I wasn't afraid.

As we got closer, I noticed fewer houses and more shops, like a sweet shop, a juice shop, and a small restaurant—the kind without walls. The church sat on our right side. It was much bigger than I had expected, with stained-glass windows. Beside it was a small manmade pond with a short bridge over it leading into a small building. We crossed the bridge, and the boys pointed at all of the pictures inside.

Above our heads were portraits of various saints, displaying their name, origin, and when they had lived. They each had a favorite, even those who weren't Christian, and they excitedly pointed them out to me. Through a window, we saw Joseph's car approach, and they scrambled to reach the church before them. We removed our shoes and left them on the steps outside the sanctuary and entered.

The church wasn't like mine at home, and I felt very odd being barefoot. It was just the sanctuary, no classrooms or offices. The stage where the priest stood was at the back, with three sections for sitting on the sides. Two of the sections featured plastic chairs, like the ones in the hostel. It appeared men mostly filled them; though our group and some wives and elderly people also sat in them. The third section contained women only, sitting on the floor in their sarees. I felt bad for them— sitting alone on the hard floor in their fancy dresses. It didn't take long to notice everyone was staring at me just as much as I was staring at them.

The announcements and sermon proved dreadfully boring since I understood about five words of Malayalam. I didn't know the songs either, but at least we got to stand during them. After what felt like fifty years, the priest gave communion—first to the men on our side then to the men on the other side and finally to the women's side.

The walk home was much less eventful than the walk to the church.

A few days later while eating breakfast and chatting cheerfully, Joseph visited the study hall room, looking very serious. "Jurnee, please come to my office when you're finished." He walked away just as suddenly and sternly as he had come.

One by one, the students at my table began questioning me. "You can't be so relaxed with us. See? You're now also in trouble."

I laughed, but part of me was afraid and tried to remember if I had done anything to warrant a reprimand. I had been joking and playing with them as peers to get them to open up more and gain confidence in speaking English, but had I gone too far at some point?

I quickly finished my food and walked down the hallway to his office.

He saw me before I could knock. "Yes, Jurnee. We got an email. Could you please reply to it?"

I had become a bit of a computer savior here, since many didn't have a lot of computer experience. When I typed, crowds would gather to see such a spectacle of someone typing ninety-five words per minute. At home, it wasn't much to be excited about, but here it made me feel like Britney Spears.

He gestured for me to sit at the laptop, and I read the email with him. It seemed a young woman from Canada had heard about the school and was interested in teaching. She was staying just a few hours away in Varkala, had related experience, and seemed like she would be a really good fit with everyone. She wanted to meet someone before coming, since it was in a village.

"Second Saturday was delayed until this weekend due to the holiday break between terms," I said. "I could go to Varkala with some of the students and meet her to see how it goes then bring her back, if she's interested in coming."

"Sounds like a great plan!" Joseph said.

Second Saturday was the second weekend of every month when the children could go home to be with their families.

I typed out a reply.

Some of the students had been asking me to visit their homes in Varkala for weeks now; it would be a great opportunity to meet their families and see a new town. Everyone said it was a beautiful beach cliff town, and I was dying to see it.

We got a response the next day. *That sounds great, Jurnee! I'll see you all then.* She ended it with her Indian number, so we could get ahold of her while we were there.

Joseph was thrilled. I was excited too, but nervous also. It would be fun to have someone to share this experience with, someone I could speak in slang with, and someone I could relate to more deeply. But, on the opposite end, what if they liked her more than me, or she was a better teacher than me? My original insecurities and fears from weeks earlier crept back.

I made a list of the students I knew were from Varkala—Sindhu, Karthik, Janaki, Radhika, Devu, and Aravind, that I knew of. Maybe there were more. I planned to speak with them about it at dinner. Where I sat for each meal was now less of an auctioneering event and now usually kept to a schedule. Eight tables with three meals per day allowed me to sit with everyone at least twice per week.

Since most of the students living in Varkala were girls, I sat at the girls table for dinner.

Sindhu started, "Jurnee Miss, what are your plans for Second Saturday?"

"Actually, I was planning to visit this place I've heard a lot about."

Every face came closer and seemed more curious. "Which place?"

"I'm not sure if you've heard of it ..."

They grew more curious and more impatient. "Jurnee Miss, we have heard of every place."

"Do you know Varkala?"

In those four words, it was as if I had lit a stick of dynamite. Squeals erupted to the point that Rizwan looked to make everything was fine.

"Jurnee Miss, you *must* come home with me."

"No, me!"

They all spoke over each other, clamoring for my attention and a commitment to stay at their house. Something I was so excited about and I couldn't wait to do now filled me with anxiety. What if I upset one of them by staying at someone else's house?

"You all decide where I stay, and I'll keep to your wishes."

There. That was final and easy.

They smiled happily and slightly maniacally at the chance to have such control. And, best of all, I didn't have to say *no* to anyone.

Second Saturday finally arrived. Devu and Aravind's parents and little brother Krishna came. He was in LKG, and they felt he was too young to live away from his parents. They would be taking me to Varkala via train. I hadn't been in an Indian train ever and not even an American train in quite a long time. After some quick introductions, we signed out on the hostel registry and bid everyone goodbye for the weekend.

Somehow the six of us piled into an auto with the adults sitting on the bench, each with a child on their lap. Luckily, Devu and Aravind were in second and fourth standard, so they could still fit relatively easily. The driver looked annoyed, but it was just until we reached the train station.

Riding through the village roads reminded me how much I loved this place. Apart from our Sunday morning walks, I had been spending all my time inside the gate, missing the cement fences, giant fruit bearing trees, farm animals roaming in yards, and brightly colored houses. It felt as though I'd been there for years. I didn't want to leave, but I was curious about this Varkala and what awaited us there. Also, *who*.

The train station was small but larger than I had expected. We approached the ticket counter, and I suddenly became nervous. What if the seats weren't assigned? What if I had to sit away from everyone and missed the stop and then was stranded alone on the train, wandering for the rest of my life?

The ticket clerk called us and spoke with their father. They completed their transaction, then the five of them walked away from the desk.

It was my turn, and I approached the desk. I started to ask the clerk how much the ticket was to Varkala, but he stopped me mid-sentence. "Madam, he has paid."

I couldn't believe the generosity. "What was the price?"

"Madam, fifty rupees."

I thanked him then quickened my pace to reach them, and we made our way to the train. Their father led the way, Devu and Aravind right behind him, his wife holding Krishna's hand behind, and myself in the back. The train rolled up as we reached the platform. It was huge, blue, and very old looking. It didn't look sleek. The numbers seemed hand painted. It looked as though it was from another time, but that was part of India's anachronistic charm.

We waited and then entered. We didn't all sit together, but we were within the same two rows, so it wasn't as scary as I had originally thought. A boy no older than eighteen walked up and down the aisle, carrying a basket of snacks over his head. Another boy came with a juice basket. A woman beside me purchased box of *biriyani* for forty rupees. I was amazed at the prices—only about fifty cents for something that would easily cost thirty times that in a restaurant back home. Despite this, she still haggled to make it lower. He refused to change the rate though.

The train squeaked and jolted slightly forward. It then rhythmically crawled until it rolled at a steady pace. The trees passed slowly then faster and faster. The warm breeze came through the windows. They didn't even have windows; it was just rectangular cutouts with metal bars. Are those called *windows*? The hostel and school buses were like that too. Even in Trivandrum, it had been common. Was there a shortage of glass?

"Jurnee Miss?" Their mother gently nudged me awake. "We reached."

I was so grateful she had woken me as I checked the time in my phone. It had only been an hour. I looked around, blinking. I found my backpack and followed her and the children off the train.

It wasn't far from the village, but everything here felt different. There were numerous foreigners so less eyes were on me; I basked in my newfound anonymity. We all got into the same auto and rode for about fifteen minutes until we reached a dirt lane. We walked down the tiny stretch until we reached a small cement structure. Their father took a key from his pocket. We were home.

Walking inside, I saw the home was very simple. The living room was about 10x10, but it was also the bedroom. A kitchen similar to the hostel in that it had a gas cylinder attached to a cook top, like at a campground, and no oven sat adjacent to the main room. I had never seen a kitchen without an oven before coming to India. I remembered my father not wanting me to ever use the oven when it was hot outside; maybe that's why no ovens were in India, because it was too hot. Or maybe because normal Indian food simply didn't require it.

Their parents were just a few years older than me, but it was strange what different lives we led. They were settled, living in a paradise with three beautiful children. I was unemployed and living with my parents. We all envied each other's lives.

The entire family had impeccable English. Their parents said it was because they come from Karnataka—a state just north of Kerala—so they weren't completely fluent in Malayalam and could manage better in English with the tourists. Even though Anooj had mentioned the language diversity earlier, I was still shocked.

We chatted for a bit before their mother came out with bowls of snacks. The first had banana chips, something I strangely loved despite hating bananas. The second had *mixture*, what I recognized from the hostel as Indian Chex Mix. The third was a rolled white thing with black dots no larger than my index finger. It seemed fried, but I hadn't seen it before. She set them on the floor between us, and we happily ate. Their mother returned to the kitchen and emerged with *chaiyya* for everyone. I learned this was what people in Kerala call *chai*.

We chatted for hours about life in the US, life in Kerala, and life in Karnataka. I loved hearing about everything but also reveled in the comfort of speaking openly in fluent English with people. I had taken communication for granted all these years. Before we knew it, the sun had set, and the children were dozing off on the floor.

Their doting mother collected blankets for everyone, and the six of us slept together on the floor. It was surprisingly comfortable, and I felt oddly close to these people I had met just hours before. Their life clearly had struggles, but they loved each other immensely. I had learned their children stay in a boarding facility, because they had difficulty paying to support them, so their father's brother in France paid for them to attend and live at school. Their family owned a small shop, but they earned their money by walking up and down the beach, selling *lungis* to tourists.

I awoke to the sound of their mother making breakfast for everyone and felt a sudden pang of homesickness as I remembered my own mother often making waffles for our breakfast. She was so happy for everyone to be together. I thought how hard it must be for them to only see their children for one weekend a month, and they were very clearly so happy to be back home with their parents and Krishna.

I helped Devu fold the blankets and put them in the corner. Devu went to the kitchen and returned with a tray of *chaiyya* for everyone. Each tiny metal cup was sat in a small metal bowl. While I blew on mine, they used the cup below to pour it in a stream from cup to cup. It was an ingenious way to quickly cool it off that Anooj had taught me in Trivandrum. Their mother brought a plate of *idli* and another plate containing what seemed to be tomato and coconut chutney.

"The food is wonderful, Mrs. Gowda."

"*Dei*. I am your *chechi* only."

"The food is wonderful, *chechi*," I replied with a smile. I loved that everyone called each other by the names of familial relations. It made me feel so close to anyone. In the US, familial terms are used only when referencing someone, with the exception of your parents and grandparents and sometimes aunts and uncles.

Devu and Aravind made no attempt to conceal how excited they were to be back with their parents and Krishna. They never stopped smiling for even a moment; they were ecstatic.

"Jurnee, would you like to have a hot bath?"

I was excited until I remembered everything was not as it seemed in India, and they probably didn't mean an actual bath. The words may be the same, but the meanings were often different. "I'd love one. Where is it?"

"Just wait two minutes. I'll get it ready." She jumped to her feet and rushed to the kitchen.

I must have looked confused, because Aravind immediately clarified, "She's making hot the water."

I felt awful and went to the kitchen. "*Chechi*, no need. Please relax."

"No, dear. Our guest is the god. I will do this for you."

Anooj had said this. Was it a common phrase?

If she made hot water for every person, it would take her the whole morning. I couldn't possibly ask this of her. "Really, *chechi*. I'll go and bathe. Devu or Aravind can use the hot water."

Her brows furrowed, and she squinted with a look of disappointment. She actually *wanted* to do this. She didn't feel compelled.

I apologized profusely. "I'll just wait there."

A smile crept across her lips, and, a moment later, she returned with a bucket similar to the one I had already seen in the bathroom, but it was metal. When she handed it to me, I realized how strong she was. I had to use both hands for what she effortlessly had carried in a single hand.

Even though it was a bucket bath, using the warm water was more comforting than the showers I had taken with the water heaters and somehow even better than the long steamy showers from home. It was luxurious.

One by one, we took turns with the hot baths as their mother made hot water for each of us. I had noticed before how excited Devu and Aravind were, but now I saw the same childlike excitement in their mother as well. They were her life.

We spent the day together having snacks, chatting and walking around the beach. It was the perfect day. In the evening, I left Devu and Aravind to have some time with their family and went to one of the restaurants on the beach to meet Sindhu, Karthik, and the Canadian. I sent a quick WhatsApp message to everyone, so they would know I had the table ready.

I also took a moment to check in with my parents and some friends back home. Everyone was posting on Facebook about how cold it was, but luckily, I didn't have that problem.

Responding to Anooj, I let him know how things were going in Varkala. I mentioned that I'd been staying with Devu and Aravind's family and that a Canadian was coming.

He said he wanted to visit me at school, but I genuinely didn't know how it was possible since I was always busy between classes and the hostel. Under any other circumstances, I would have loved to, but it was imperative that I do well here. My entire future was riding on this experience.

CHAPTER 6

The restaurant reminded me of one I had been to once in Florida. The chairs were made of a brown wicker, and the tables had glass tops, but they matched. It wasn't fully enclosed, so they could utilize the beach view to their advantage. The Canadian arrived first.

"Jurnee?" she asked hesitantly as she approached the table.

"Hi! It's so good to meet you. Mellissa, right? How was your trip?"

"I've been here for a while, but so far everything has been great. How long have you been at St. Joseph?"

"A couple months and I absolutely love it. Everyone is so nice."

"And you said some of the students will be joining us? I've actually been staying with a new friend of mine. Aditya. He's a local here."

"That's great! Have you been enjoying your time here so far?" I was curious to know how another North American was faring in Kerala.

"Yeah, it's a lot of fun. I'm just looking for a little change of scenery. I want to get the full experience while I'm here."

"It's definitely a new experience. I've never been happier. I absolutely love it at the school."

Just then, Sindhu and Karthik came.

Mellissa and I stood to greet them.

"Sindhu! So good to see you. Karthik, how is your shop?" I asked as I hugged Sindhu. As the oldest girl in the hostel, it always felt like we were more peers than student/teacher. I had really missed her presence this past few days.

Sindhu didn't waste a moment. "You are Mellissa, the Canadian?"

"Yes."

"But you have a pinch of Chinese. Are you from China?"

"My father's family comes from China."

"Wow! Have you been to China?" Sindhu was enthralled by the Canadian. I was now chopped liver.

"Do you know Chinese?" Karthik joined the interrogation.

"Actually, no to both."

"What is your job?" Sindhu continued.

"I'm a social media manager for an amusement park."

Excitement leapt across the table. "Did you have to study for that?"

"I studied biology."

Their faces went from excitement to confusion. I decided to change the subject. "So, what brought you to India?"

"I've travelled across Southeast Asia a bit and decided to try India once. I have winters off since it's off season, so I travel someplace warm."

It was genius. I briefly thought about giving up teaching.

We continued chatting and decided the next evening we would travel back together to spend one last day seeing the sights of Varkala. That had been the intention, but really we just spent the day on the beach.

That evening, they ran up to the car Mellissa's friend had hired for all of us but past me. To Mellissa. *She's new, and they're curious,* I consoled myself.

They writhed about her in excitement. She was new and shiny, as I had been just a month prior. The children asked the same questions we had discussed at dinner the evening prior and a few more.

Joseph came out to welcome her and to give her the same introduction to things as I had.

The rest of us dispersed to put our things in our rooms and then headed to the study hall room for dinner. It was late, but the evening prayers began as I entered. The prayers ended and dinner progressed as usual, apart from an added guest. She sat at the girls table, and I sat at with the fifth and sixth standard boys. They had become some of my best friends.

After dinner, I noticed Mellissa still had her bags with her. "Should I show you to your room? Do you need a lock?"

"I have the lock, and I don't have any problem unlocking it, but it won't lock."

I remembered how difficult it had been for me my first few times. These old-style locks were no joke. Like a pro, I showed her how to lock it. It wasn't automatic, as our padlocks were back home; you had to turn the key while holding the lock in a locked position.

She was just as amazed as I had been the first time someone had done it for me and showered me with gratitude.

I helped her with her bags as we went upstairs for the evening.

The next morning at school, Nissy Miss called Mellissa forward in the assembly. We stood in the back corner of the courtyard between the LKG and UKG classrooms, and I could see her eyeing the door.

"Not a fan of public speaking?" I asked her.

"I hate it." She looked at me nervously.

"Do you want me to come with you?" I was equally afraid of being in front of people, but somehow, when needing to comfort someone else, my fears evaporated.

"Would you?" Relief washed across her face.

"Of course." I was happy to help, remembering how stressful my first day had been, totally away from everyone and everything familiar, the vastly different dialect of English, the unspoken rules. It was a lot to take in.

We walked around the courtyard together until we reached the front of the assembly.

Mellissa meandered to Nissy Miss and the microphone, glancing over her shoulder at me in the back corner of the stage before speaking. "Good morning, everyone. My name is Mellissa, and I am from Canada.

I'll be helping with your English program for the next couple weeks, and I'm happy to meet you all." She passed the microphone to Nissy Miss and began to walk away.

"Thank you, Mellissa Miss," Nissy Miss called into the microphone. "Now please share with us a song."

Mellissa looked at me and froze, like a deer stuck in the headlights. "I couldn't possibly." She chuckled to Nissy Miss.

I was confused. Why did they want her to sing?

"Don't be modest, dear. Just sing one song."

I couldn't just stand there. I remembered how she felt when they had asked her to sing in the hostel last night suddenly after dinner. It was clear she had been wildly uncomfortable. "We'll both sing a song!"

Mellissa smiled sheepishly and whispered, "But which song? I can't think of any."

"Just move your mouth. I'll sing," I whispered.

We headed to the front as I began the only song I could think of—"Santeria" by Sublime. I'm not sure why or how it popped into my head as I shyly sang out the lyrics.

Everyone smiled and whispered to each other. I remembered Mohan Sir telling me they hadn't heard foreign songs sung in real life before; they were probably excited and not laughing *at* me.

Mellissa stood beside me, lip synching.

As I reached the last two lines before the chorus, I'd forgotten the lyrics may not be child friendly. Hopefully no one noticed. I powered through the catchy singalong-worthy chorus—probably off key—then stopped; it was hardly the whole song, but I didn't want to sing the whole song. I had already probably messed up half the words anyway.

The entire room clapped for my poorly sung and deeply inappropriate song as I passed the microphone to Nissy Miss. "What a beautiful song by our Jurnee Miss and Mellissa Miss!"

"Mellissa Miss will be joining some of your classes today. Please give her a warm welcome and listen to her the way you've been listening to Jurnee Miss," Joseph continued but switched to Malayalam.

After Joseph had dismissed the assembly, I went to my regularly scheduled classes, and Mellissa followed Nissy Miss into the office to make her schedule. It was so odd how after just a month here I was comfortable and established enough to help someone else settle in. I really felt I belonged here.

It wasn't long before Mellissa and I were good friends. It was fun to be the *Anooj* to someone else. I helped her with word equivalents, tasted the food before her to see if it was too spicy and helped her remember peoples' names. I also helped her assimilate better. The teachers would come to me with their concerns, and it was my responsibility to convey them to her. It was usually a small issue with what she was wearing or the one time she cursed.

It all went smoothly though. I wasn't sure what I had been so jealous of in the beginning. She fit in perfectly, and things felt more like home when she was here. One of my college friends had said to me once he always felt more at home when he heard his accent, but I had never known what it meant until I met the Canadian. Sure, it was slightly different, but it made me less homesick.

We taught older classes together, doing improv skits with each other to display examples of different grammatical rules. We taught younger classes together, acting out "I'm a Little Teapot" and "Itsy-Bitsy Spider." Mellissa reminded me of "Hickory Dickory Dock," so we did that as well. The children loved our classes, and their eyes lit up whenever they saw it was our turn to be in their room. We felt like celebrities.

One weekend afternoon, we even left the hostel on our own. It was my first time leaving the school grounds without a local. We found a highly rated restaurant nearby called Hotel Aaryas and asked Sindhu if she knew how to get ahold of Ishar, one of the bus drivers who owned an auto.

She went to speak with Cook Auntie for a moment and then emerged with a phone number.

It was exhilarating to be on our own. While walking into the restaurant, I heard a shrill shouting. I turned and saw a woman leaning from her auto, pointing at us and bellowing, "*Madhaama!*"

For a moment, I was worried and turned to Mellissa. "Was she talking to us?" Everyone on the road had turned and now gawked at us.

A man who had been outside and overheard told us it meant a white foreign woman and wasn't offensive, that she was just making a loud observation.

We thanked him and continued inside.

At the restaurant, we ate *dosa* and *chaiyya*, and shared a few appetizers. The best part? The total was less than five dollars. It was incredible and absolutely delicious. I could live here comfortably forever without depleting my savings, and I briefly contemplated it.

We spent time chatting about everything that had transpired and how sad we were that she would be leaving soon. It had been so much fun these past ten days, and now she was leaving just as suddenly as she had come. It was just a tourism destination for her, so she wanted to move to the next location.

The next morning at school, the faculty cancelled classes for a surprise going-away party for her instead. The teachers all wore really nice sarees, some looked to be fine silk and others had beads and sequins stitched onto them. The male teachers wore their usual slacks and button-down shirts.

The assembly began the same as always. We had the band, the welcoming, and the pledge. But then Nissy Miss and Joseph approached the microphone.

"Good morning, students," Nissy Miss began. "Today, we celebrate our Mellissa Miss as she leaves to go back to Canada."

"She has been a great asset to us, and we will remember her dearly," Joseph added.

"Mellissa Miss," Nissy Miss called as she motioned her hand downward to beckon her. "A few words to our students please."

Mellissa still didn't like speaking in front of people, but now they weren't strangers. "I've so enjoyed being with all of you these past few days, and I've probably learned more from you than you've learned from me. It's been so great getting to know all of you, and I can't thank you enough." She glanced at me when she finished with, "I'll miss all of you."

I would really miss her too.

Nissy Miss continued, "Will the next program please come to the front."

Group by group, the students entertained us with singing, dancing, and some short skits. We didn't understand a word, since it was in Malayalam, but we didn't clap any less enthusiastically. They did a great job, and it was a really thoughtful farewell.

Before we knew it, it was lunchtime and school was dismissed. Mellissa hugged everyone goodbye as we headed to the hostel for her final meal with us. The hostel students were noticeably morose. She had been a big part of our hostel life, and we were sad to see her go. Cook Auntie called an auto for her, and we joined the tables together to avoid bickering over who could eat with her. After eating and a few selfies, her car arrived. We walked her outside and waved as she drove away.

We walked sullenly back to the hostel. It felt empty without her. I didn't think I could like someone so much after just a couple weeks.

"Jurnee Miss?" Nelson and some of the others came behind me. "You don't want to go."

"I'll have to eventually."

"No, you don't. You can live here with us. We will find someone for you to marry, and your children can study here."

"What about my family?"

"Miss. *We* are your family," Radhika interjected.

They were so sweet, I almost cried. I had met a lot of people in my life, but no one had made me feel as accepted and beloved as these children. "I'll think about it." The logistics couldn't be too hard. Or maybe I could meet someone and get an Indian green card that way. It could happen.

They all smiled, and we went inside.

Rizwan returned from speaking with the security guard. "MD Sir will be gone a while. What do you all want to do?"

I could see in their faces how much they were pondering. With such carefully structured lives, they looked so happy to have a few free hours. It was eventually decided to have free time and then join together at 4:30 p.m. for the normal sports time.

The children went to play in their rooms. A couple of them invited me along, but I decided to catch up on my messages and maybe take a nap. I had fallen far behind on messages since I'd been so busy. I had never expected that a volunteer project would consume all twenty-four hours of the day. I loved it, but I had no personal time.

I sent a quick update to my parents and posted a recent group selfie to placate my friends.

I saw Anooj's message. *Jurnee! I have a big surprise for you.*

I tried to think what it could possibly be, but I had no idea. *Give me a hint!*

You'll see soon enough.

But my thoughts were disrupted when Krishna and Naveen ran to my door. "Jurnee Miss! Jurnee Miss!" they shouted, knocking fervently.

Worried, I leapt from bed and opened the door. "Is everything okay?"

"We found a baby pigeon! You must come!"

They didn't even give me a moment to collect myself or to lock the door. Each took a hand and led me upstairs, running the whole way. The floor was filthy on the third and fourth floors, since they weren't used, and I really wished I had gotten my flip flops. I was a little annoyed but mostly curious. Where was this baby pigeon they were so excited about?

We went all the way to the top of the stairwell, and they showed me a small nest in the corner. They picked up the pigeon despite my protests. "That isn't safe. It may have diseases."

"Jurnee Miss, don't be so afraid of everything. It's just a baby," Krishna said as he brought his hands holding the bird closer to my face.

I was terrified but fascinated. It was small and … yellow? That couldn't be a pigeon, but who was I to question the local wildlife?

"Pet her, Jurnee Miss."

Sure, they misbehaved sometimes, but these boys were so sweet and gentle with the bird. I decided to trust them and gently petted the bird on its head. "What will we name her?"

"Let's call her *Mellissa*."

"Super idea," I added. I hoped the *super* wasn't too much. I had heard it said a lot around here.

We sat and admired the bird for a moment before I noticed the stairs continued higher. "Where does this lead?" I gestured with a turn of my face, like a true local.

"The roof," they answered in unison, like it was the silliest thing I could have asked.

Naveen stood and beckoned the both of us to follow.

Up one more flight of stairs led us to the most breathtaking site I had seen. We were above the treetops, and all I could see was greenery for miles against the blue sky, with colorful houses sprinkled between. Each day, something new left me breathless.

The next morning when I went to Nissy Miss's office for my daily schedule, I noticed I had Ananya Miss's library class. I loved spending time with the students, but she was one of my favorite teachers, and I loved catching up with her whenever I could. She was the only teacher younger than me, and we always got along really well.

When I got to Ananya Miss's class period, I was happily surprised to see it was Bhoomi Miss's day to be there. I had the choice of helping Ananya Miss oversee students reading or watch Bhoomi Miss conduct karate classes. I had heard Bhoomi Miss taught karate but hadn't gotten a chance to see it for myself. They pronounced it *kuh-raw-tay*, which was strange, but they were extremely disciplined. They all wore white karate uniforms and colored belts.

"Jurnee Miss, would you like to try?"

"Sure. Sounds like fun." I joined her on the other side of the room. "What do I do?"

"First, you want to stand with your feet apart, like mine." She gestured to her feet which were shoulder-width apart. "Then you want to push your right hand in a fist, very strong with straight arm, and pull your left hand in a fist to your side facing upwards. Like this." She demonstrated this simple movement and then did the opposite, extending her left fist while bringing her right fist to her side.

It looked easy enough, so I stood straight and did my best to make the quick motions as she had done. I thought I had done it correctly, but even Ananya Miss was laughing.

Bhoomi Miss tried to correct me, but I was hopeless. My movements weren't sharp enough, and I probably looked like a psycho.

"Okay, let's try some other basic movements."

We tried a side kick and some general karate chops. They were equal failures, and I was clearly wasting their class time.

"Why don't you both have a karate match?" Ananya Miss suggested from across the room.

I looked to Bhoomi Miss, unsure about it, but the room was soon flooded with deafening cheers. It seems it had already been decided; we would fight.

"Ready, Jurnee Miss?" Bhoomi Miss asked.

I meekly smiled and nodded in the uncertain sideways style.

"Okay, get into position," she said as she demonstrated how I should stand. "And begin."

I didn't know what to do. What if I hurt her?

She sensed my hesitation. "Don't worry about hurting me. I am very experienced. I have been studying this since I was just a girl, and it has made me very strong. That is why I started teaching this for the young students, so I could help protect all, but especially our girl children." It was such a sweet thought. She was so selfless. "I will be fine. It is you who should be worried, not me," she added with a wink.

I wasn't sure if she was being serious or teasing me, but I stood as she had told me and swung my arm in a karate chop.

She anticipated my move and used her forearm to block it.

I made my left hand into a low fist from what I had learned in the first lesson and extended it to her left abdomen.

That was equally unsuccessful because she simply sidestepped and blocked it with her other forearm. She was so fast.

I tried a few more methods, but everything failed. I was getting winded, but she remained calm and unfazed. She was incredible. "I surrender."

The class laughed, and she directed me to fold my hands, and we bowed to each other, like I had seen in the movies.

One of the smallest girls in the class approached me. "Good attempt, Jurnee Miss. You will learn in time."

I definitely wasn't the next karate kid.

CHAPTER 7

For the past few weeks, everyone had been talking about Annual Day. I remembered seeing it in the pictures in the school office, and I had seen many students rehearsing, but I still wasn't sure what it was all about.

It was apparently a thing every school in India did, kind of like a talent show with skits, singing, and dancing. But, best of all, teachers have to wear matching sarees. They were purple with a gold stripe, and I could not wait. I'd been admiring them from afar for weeks, and now I finally got to wear one myself.

After weeks of preparations by the students and teachers, Annual Day finally came. It was on Valentine's Day, so a lot of excitement hung in the air. When we went outside, several people were on the grounds. Piles upon piles of plastic chairs lined the soccer field in front of the small stage, and men worked to erect a canopy tent in front of it. Teachers milled about in and around the school, and students played in the playground. It wasn't set to begin until 4:30, but everyone gathered behind the badminton net near the flagpole.

"Jurnee Miss!" a few voices called to me. "It is starting now! Come!"

I wasn't sure what exactly was starting, but I followed. As I manuevered through the small crowd, the occasional voice called, "Good Morning, miss!" I wished them all a reciprocal *Good morning*, until I saw Joseph motioning to me to join him just behind the flagpole.

"Good morning, Jurnee. Since Annual Day is tonight, we must now do the flag hoisting."

"Oh! That's great!" I said as I looked up to see a flag tied in a ball making its way to the top of the pole.

One string pulled it up the pole and another held the ball together. When the flag reached the top, Rizwan pulled the second string, and the flag opened, showering us with flower petals, and they sang the national anthem. We all clapped, and Joseph gave a short speech about Annual Day and how it was a great representation of all the work of the teachers and students.

"Jurnee Miss, come to help us decorate," Nissy called.

I followed her with the other teachers to the front of the school where I saw a giant chalk outline reading, *13ᵗʰ Annual Day*, as well as some outlines of stars. Everyone filled them in with flower petals. It was clear how much effort had gone into it, and it looked beautiful.

Smitha handed me a short lamp like the one that had been given to Mellissa at her farewell party and directed me to place it in the center of the petals on one of the stars.

When the students got bored and threw petals at each other, we divided into teams. One team was to complete the decorations for the front steps. One team was to decorate the entryway. One team was to decorate the stage. One team was to set up the chairs. Since chairs were the easiest job, it was mostly comprised of fourth to eighth standard hostel students, and they selected me to oversee them.

I ensured the lines were straight, the aisle was wide enough, they didn't disturb the workers who had come to set up the tent, and that they stayed focused. Everyone was so excited it was difficult to keep everyone on task.

"Jurnee Miss, will you do any song?" Radhika asked. "I saw your name on the list, but it didn't say what you would be doing."

"My name? Are you sure?" I hadn't signed up for anything. She was one of the hosts though, so she had a master list of the programs. Should I be worried?

"Don't worry, miss." She could probably feel my anxiety from across the aisle.

I had heard about a thousand would be in attendance tonight. I was not going in front of anyone.

Radhika changed the subject. "Look at the new stage decorations. Aren't they grand?"

A dark red skirt covered the stage's concrete foundation that matched the stage walls. The back wall, however, had a ruched golden sheet covering it, and it looked like a professional production. I recognized Ajitha Miss and Raina Miss hanging the banner across the back with some balloons. The curtain was a beautiful shade of blue, and it was no wonder everyone was so excited. This was the event of the year.

Nissy, Raina, and Ananya came behind me. "Jurnee Miss, it is getting late. We will dress you in your saree."

I was finally going to wear a saree. Every day the teachers wore them, and they always looked so elegant and perfect. Now it was my turn.

"Do you have all of the pieces? Saree, blouse, and petticoat?"

I remembered Ajitha Miss giving me a cloth bag that contained three articles of clothing, but I hadn't been able to make out what she had said about them. I didn't realize that she had given me my first saree. "I believe so."

"Go and take head bath, wear the blouse and petticoat, then give a missed call, and we will come," Nissy directed.

I remembered that *head bath* meant washing your hair, nodded in agreement and went inside. This was it.

The petticoat was strange—just a large cloth and a drawstring made into a makeshift skirt. A quick Google showed me that I was to tie it as tight as I could at the smallest point of my waist. The blouse was essentially a designer crop top. I thought the clasps would go in the back, but my Google search showed it was to go in front, so the saree would cover it.

I looked at myself in the mirror and felt strange. I had never worn clothes with an open stomach, and now, here I was, the top half fancy and the bottom half extremely plain. I called Nissy, let it ring once then hung up. No one here called each other; they just gave missed calls. I couldn't get over how odd it was, no matter how many times I participated in it.

About ten minutes later, they knocked on my door. I stood meekly to the side with arms crossed, never having had to stand in front of anyone in this state.

"Jurnee Miss," Nissy said with a confused chuckle. "I never thought a foreigner will be so shy."

Raina and Ananya also expressed confusion as Ananya came behind me to put my hair into a bun, so it would stay out of the way. Nissy checked to see that my blouse and petticoat were correct, and Raina placed a large plastic box with several small compartments onto my desk. It resembled a tackle box that my dad had when I was a kid.

They began. Nissy unfolded the saree to find the correct end and tucked it into the petticoat below where my right elbow fell. She tucked it across my stomach and to the other side then instructed me to turn as she continued tucking. Once she had completed one full round, she took the loose saree around me another time and put it over my shoulder. She adjusted it a few times before determining the length she liked then pleated and took a safety pin from Raina's box to pin into the top of the blouse's left sleeve. She was careful not to poke me in the process, for which I was very thankful.

After we had settled the hanging part, she pulled it around and behind my torso and tucked it into the side. I was now left with a mountain of fabric hanging from the front of the petticoat. Nissy pleated it extraordinarily fast and secured it with more safety pins before and after tucking in the final piece. She unpinned the part she had pinned to my left sleeve and pulled it back up and around.

After she re-pinned it, I looked at the three of them to see what they thought.

"Jurnee Miss! You look beautiful."

"*Sundhari!*"

"Super, miss!"

Now that they had approved my dress, Ananya combed my hair.

They all spoke in Malayalam, but it sounded more like an argument.

I understood from their gestures they were engaged in a heated debate of whether I would have my hair braided or have it half up and half down. I didn't understand a word, but it seemed they had come to a compromise, because Ananya was braiding tiny bits of hair from behind my ears to join together at the back with a string of jasmine flowers on top. Unanimous approval came again, and it was Raina's turn to place jewelry.

"Wait," Nissy Miss said. "Something is missing."

"You're right. She has no *kajal*," Raina said.

I had worn just some light foundation to keep my skin tone even and mascara with lip balm.

She removed a jar of what looked like nail polish from the box. She painted the top of my eyelid with it, and I was startled by how cold it was. When the chill subsided, she told me to open my eyes as she put a black pencil on the ridge of skin above my bottom lashes. The three of them inspected me again to ensure nothing else was missing.

"Okay, now fine," Nissy confirmed.

Raina again retrieved some costume jewelry from the box that matched a saree—a purple pendant on a golden chain with matching long purple earrings. She placed a teardrop-shaped *bindi* between my eyebrows and pinned a ribbon to the saree's front, indicating I was one of the esteemed guests. A small collection of purple and golden bangles were divided between my two wrists.

"Jurnee Miss, you are like a Barbie doll," Ananya said as the others chuckled.

I certainly felt like one, with everyone dressing me.

"Please be very careful, because if the dress spoils, we may not be available to fix it," Nissy warned.

I realized that I was wearing a long piece of fabric secured entirely by safety pins and was suddenly terrified.

Following the teachers back to school, I was praised by all. Every single person we passed told me how great I looked. I didn't feel very confident, since I had never worn a saree before, but, by the time we reached the school, the compliments had overtaken my fears.

"Jurnee Miss! Come meet my mom!" Nassir shouted from the tent.

I learned that his entire family had travelled from Trivandrum to see his dance tonight.

"Jurnee Miss, please accept our gift to you." His mother handed me a box that read, *Plum Cake*. "Nassir told us about your problem with the rice and how much you love cake. We don't want you to be hungry. Call us anytime you need something."

I couldn't believe how thoughtful they were. I felt bad they knew I had been struggling with the rice, but it was such a kind gesture.

"You're so cute, Jurnee Miss. Not at all like other foreigners."

"What do you mean?"

"The other foreigners. They all wear less dress and flirt with boys and speak badly. But you have the heart of a *Malayali*."

I wasn't sure if I should be thankful or mildly offended, but I assumed she had good intentions. "Thank you, *chechi*."

"No saying thank you to us. We are your family."

I offered to cut it, so we could all have it together, but she rejected my offer. "This is for you only. Keep it in your room and come."

I nodded and headed to the hostel, careful not to do anything to ruin the integrity of the safety pins … or of me.

Winston and Andriya entered the hostel as I left. "Jurnee Miss, Nissy Miss calling. Mellissa Miss has come, and the chief guest will arrive soon."

"Mellissa came back? I thought she returned to Canada."

"She is here only."

"Great! Thanks, guys," I said as we all walked out together toward the front of the school. Since I had been inside getting dressed during most of the decorating, I hadn't seen how nicely it turned out. Streamers were draped along the drive. Long strands of lights and garlands hung from the top of the school building. Everyone was lined in front of the school and looked incredible.

The band kids wore uniforms with their instruments; roller skating kids donned their skates and uniforms; karate kids were dressed in their white uniforms and colored belts, and I stood at the side with the teachers in our matching purple sarees. At the very front of the group were three girls in, what I had recognized to be, traditional outfits. They wore all white with gold borders. The portion between their legs wasn't a skirt but rather cloth pleated tightly, like an accordion. There appeared to be a built-in skirt lying over the pants, and together with the pleats, they made a unique but beautiful style. They wore heavy black eyeliner and golden belts with elaborately decorated hair.

Mellissa stood beside Nissy in a matching purple saree. I waved to her as I quickened my pace.

"Is everything okay? You just left a few days ago," I asked worriedly.

"Everything is fine. I just wanted to see this Annual Day event everyone was talking about. I leave India next weekend."

"Oh cool." I felt stupid for assuming she had left India just because she had left the school. "How did you know to get a purple saree?"

"Nissy Miss told me," she said as she turned and smiled at her.

Nissy Miss's son David ran over. "Your dress is very good, *Madhaama Chechi*."

My heart melted hearing this. He considered me his foreigner elder sister. "Thank you, David. Yours is good too!"

He was dressed to match the other boys in his class for their group dance.

Before he could return to his place, a car arrived. The gate opened as whispers grew to talking and then to shouting.

Rizwan hollered to calm everyone before the chief guest entered.

Smitha nodded at him in gratitude, and everyone took their positions.

Teachers had given flowers to a few select children to present to the chief guest—a television comedian—and everyone knew him well.

Joseph, Nissy, and Smitha led his entourage into Joseph's office.

Mellissa joined us, and we all sat at Joseph's desk as they distributed snacks and *chaiyya*.

They spoke in Malayalam, so we chatted amongst ourselves in English.

"Where have you been staying? Are you still with Aditya?"

"Yeah, we've been hanging out still at Varkala. I just love being there. It's such a beautiful place. I think I may come back next year too."

"You have to! I was thinking of coming back next year too. It would be so much fun to team up again."

"It would! We have to stay in touch."

I was about to agree, but we had gotten too loud, and the staff interrupted us. We silently smirked to one another, like our own students when we scolded them, and sat silently so as not to disturb the others. After they finished speaking, they placed us in special chairs just below the stage. The students and their families sat behind in the plastic chairs while we sat in firm chairs with a long table.

It was the beginning of the program, so we waited through a series of speeches. Joseph, Nissy, and the chief guest each gave a speech in a little bit of English, but they were mostly in Malayalam to allow everyone to understand.

I looked longingly behind me. How much I had been looking forward to meeting their families and spending this time with the students, and I would be sitting here silently at the front of the crowd.

Mellissa had the same feeling, so we excused ourselves to get something to eat. We walked about two hundred yards to the school building and met several of the students' parents on the way. I was happy to see Devu and Aravind's family again.

"*Chechi*!" I exclaimed as I hugged their mom. "This is Mellissa from Canada."

"Welcome, Mellissa," she said with a smile. As she turned, she noticed Devu and Aravind were no longer behind her. "I'll just go and come."

I began walking toward our seats when Mellissa stopped me. "Aren't you going to wait for her?" She sounded concerned.

"She's not coming back." I had officially learned this new dialect of English.

Everyone was dressed nicely; the decorations were perfect; the hostel kids were over the moon to be with their families; the regular students were excited for their parents to see their performances, and the older students were happy to have an excuse to spend Valentine's Day with their crushes.

When we reached our seats, Nissy was oddly stern. "Jurnee Miss, where have you been?"

"We just went to get some food," I said as we held up our snacks.

"Your speech is coming next. Go behind and let Mary Miss know you're ready."

"My speech?"

"Yes, dear. You are representing our English department. We mentioned it last week."

I scanned the crowd and saw hundreds of people. My stomach dropped. I could feel my face reddening.

"Don't be afraid. Most of them are not fluent in English. It doesn't matter what you say. Just speak from your heart and introduce yourself."

With a deep breath, a smile from Nissy, and a thumbs up from Mellissa, I turned and meandered to the back of the stage. Once there, I immediately spotted Mary Miss. Her saree pleats were always sharp and perfect, hair always in a low ponytail, and she had the kindest smile.

"Mary Miss?"

"Yes. You will be next. Are you ready?" She saw the terror in my eyes. "Don't take tension." She smiled as she guided me toward the curtain.

I was totally unprepared to speak in front of basically a million people, but I couldn't do anything about it now. All I could do was take a deep breath and walk out on stage.

The lights were bright. Hot and bright. But luckily so bright that I could barely see the crowd. Radhika and Sindhu were also onstage, since they were the hosts, so it was slightly less terrifying. Either way, there was no going back now.

Approaching the microphone, I smiled sheepishly to the crowd. "Good evening, everyone."

There was no response. This clearly wasn't an interactive crowd, so I continued. "My name is Jurnee, and I am from America, near a city called Chicago. Back home, I just completed my bachelor's degree in teaching, and it is my greatest passion. A few months ago, my mother was speaking to Joseph Sir, and the opportunity arose for me to spend some time here and gain experience teaching in a new setting. I have been here for several weeks now and can honestly say my time here has been the greatest in my life. I feel incredibly honored to have been welcomed so graciously by everyone, and I no longer feel like a foreigner. This is my home."

The crowd applauded, and I waved to them before stepping from the podium.

Radhika and Sindhu smiled to confirm I didn't blow it.

The speech was a bit more sentimental than I had wanted it to be, but, for making it up on the spot, it wasn't the worst.

Backstage, everyone said I had done a great job. It looked like the speeches were finished, and it was time for the performances to begin. The three girls from the front of the gate stepped onto the stage.

I walked around to the side to watch their dance, but a familiar face greeted me. "Anooj! What are you doing here?"

"I heard about your Annual Day and wanted to attend. The *real* question is, why you didn't invite me?"

"I thought it would be boring for you. How did you hear about a small school event happening in a village hours away from you?" I asked accusingly yet jokingly. I was happy to see him, but this definitely wasn't a coincidence. Wait. Was this his surprise?

He looked side to side, seemingly embarrassed. "Okay, I admit it. I follow your school's Facebook page, and they mentioned it."

I couldn't help but to smile. I wasn't expecting to see him at all, and I was so happy to have some time to catch up. I knew all eyes were on me though, so I had to take care to not stand too closely to him and give the wrong impression.

As we passed Mellissa, she was intrigued and immediately stood to join us. "Jurnee! You did so well on your speech! Everyone was saying so."

"Thanks. It was only mildly terrifying."

"No, definitely. I can't imagine speaking in front of this many people. I could barely speak at an assembly."

I had almost forgotten to introduce them. "Mellissa, this is my friend Anooj from Trivandrum. Anooj, this is Mellissa who came from Canada to teach for a bit."

They exchanged pleasantries, and we bought some juice. The current performance featured some of the older boys lip syncing to what I assumed to be a movie dialogue. The entire audience roared with laughter, but Mellissa and I had no idea what they were saying, so we laughed weakly to fit in.

We stood toward the back of the seating area, watching the performances and chatting with each other. Somehow Anooj had never visited Varkala, so Mellissa briefed him on all the fun things to do there. We compared our lives in India, the US, and Canada. We discussed our families and our jobs and how we felt about Kerala.

As we walked to the garbage to throw away our bottles, from nowhere, it downpoured. My hair, my saree, everything was ruined. Luckily the people sitting below the tent were still dry, but everyone else was soaked. We were all shocked, but I sensed the disappointment fall across the children who were yet to perform.

We ran to take shelter in the school where we had bought the snacks. I was devastated that I now looked like a drowned rat, and Mellissa seemed equally dismayed. Despite this, something made Anooj laugh uncontrollably. It was contagious, and we couldn't help but to laugh also.

"What are you laughing at?" I asked him.

"What are *you* laughing at, Jurnee Miss?"

"You tell me, Anooj Sir."

"It's a secret," he said with a shy smile.

Something about him in a *mundu* made him seem completely different, more handsome, and I wondered why so many men opted to wear jeans instead. Water dripped from his hair, and he pushed it back with a smile, the same way he had done the first night we had met. I caught myself staring and looked away.

Some of the younger girls who had been taking shelter with us asked us to do the hand clap game I had taught them when I had first arrived. Mellissa and I taught Anooj, so he could play also. It seemed this was the new Annual Day program.

Everyone whispered in Malayalam, a mixture of sounding cross yet disappointed. Anooj translated for us. "The parents are angry that they took time to come here, and many haven't yet seen their kids perform, but now their costumes are spoiled."

Mellissa and I looked to each other. "That's awful," we said almost in unison.

The faculty arranged to try to get everyone inside the school and get cleaned up then resume performances. We were already behind schedule and now even more so. It was almost 10 p.m., and the children were noticeably tired, but they didn't want to give up. Workers gathered tarps from upstairs, as volunteers used them to run across the field and escort those taking shelter at the stage.

The teachers had assigned the children classrooms where they could get cleaned up. It wasn't long before the performances had resumed and, despite the original disappointment in the air, all the students looked great and were ready to begin.

After a while, the rain cleared, and Anooj tapped me on the shoulder as he stood. "I'd better get started before it gets too late."

"Are you sure?" It had been so nice to hang out again. I knew he had a long drive ahead of him, but I wanted him to stay just a while longer.

"It was good seeing you again. Don't forget to call anytime, and I'll come."

"Thank you, Anooj. Let me know when you get home."

"Sure, of course."

I stood to walk him to his car.

"Stay here, see your students. No need to escort me. Imagine the scandal of their beloved Jurnee Miss walking alone with a boy in the dark."

Mellissa and I chuckled before she stood. "I'll come too. That way it'll be three."

"No, no. You both stay. It was nice to meet you, Mellissa Miss. Jurnee Miss, lovely as always." And with a flash of a smile, he was gone.

Mellissa sat and, as soon as soon as he was out of earshot, whispered, "Okay, who was *that*?"

"Anooj."

"I got that much, but clearly he is more than just *Anooj*. Spill."

I chortled. "There's nothing to spill. We met in Trivandrum, and he's been helping me fit in and understand things."

She raised an eyebrow. "Nothing more?"

"Nothing more."

"So, you don't mind if I ask you for his phone number?"

For some reason, this bothered me. "What about Aditya?"

"Just testing. Are you sure nothing is going on between you two?"

"Positive."

She didn't believe me, but we diverted our attention again to the programs. They all did so well, but I had no idea there were this many. They continued well past midnight, and parents continued to greet Mellissa and me as the evening progressed.

Sajith, one of the older boys in the hostel, approached us with his family. "Jurnee Miss, these are my parents and my sister Sajitha."

Mellissa and I stood to greet them. "Nice to meet you," we said as we reached to shake their hands.

But, at the same time, they had folded their hands. We quickly noticed our mistake and folded our hands in unison. Difference in culture.

"How are you enjoying our Kerala?" Sajith's father asked.

"It's beautiful," I said.

"The people are wonderful," Mellissa added.

"Do come stay with us some time to get a real Kerala experience," Sajitha proposed as she looked to me.

"I'd love to."

"Come tonight," their father said. "Second Saturday, no one here."

"Are you sure?" I had totally forgotten about Second Saturday, and it was really short notice.

"You must come. Go and confirm with Joseph Sir."

I looked at Mellissa to make sure it was fine, but she nodded me forward as I stood to look for Joseph. It seemed the event was nearly finished. The only families remaining were those with children yet to perform, so it wasn't difficult to spot him.

"Joseph Sir," I said as I approached.

"Jurnee! I trust you're enjoying the event?"

"Definitely. It's been an incredible experience. Sajith and Sajitha's parents have invited me to their home for the weekend. Is it okay?"

"Sure, of course. Have a good time."

"Thank you, sir. I'll see you Monday morning." I turned to let the hostel students know I was leaving, but most of them had already left with their families. I finally made it back to Mellissa. "How will you get back to Varkala? It's very late."

"My driver is here." She pointed to a man eating ice cream at the back of the room.

"Oh, good. Let me know when you reach." With that, I remembered telling Anooj to let me know when he had reached, so I checked my phone. I realized it hadn't been long though, so he couldn't possibly be home yet.

"Chatting with *Anooj*?"

I laughed with an eye roll.

"I'd better get going though. It's quite late. I hope this isn't the last time we meet," she said as she hugged me.

"Me too. Please keep in touch." People say it often, but I genuinely meant it.

As she waved goodbye and headed to her driver, I waved and approached Sajith's family. I was nervous to leave campus but knew it would be okay after having had a great experience staying with Devu and Aravind's family.

CHAPTER 8

With great enthusiasm, Sajith and Sajitha led the way to the car. She seemed to be just slightly older than he was, but they almost looked to be twins. As we crossed the road to the dirt parking lot, I thought about how much I loved today. We had played all morning; my saree was beautiful and didn't fall off. I somehow had delivered a speech in front of a thousand people, and even Anooj came. I exhaustedly climbed into the car. It'd been a while since I'd been in one. Sajith and Sajitha spoke to their mother in Malayalam. I assumed it was about breakfast, since I heard them say *dosa* and *idli*. Everything else melted into a swarm of sounds that lulled me to sleep.

"Jurnee, we have reached." I heard it clearly, but I didn't know who said it.

I looked out the window and couldn't believe my eyes. Their house was gorgeous and so much bigger than I had imagined. The other houses I'd seen near this village were mostly constructed with cement bricks and were no more than one or two rooms in total. The gate was ornate iron, and bushes and trees were everywhere. I only wished it were daytime, so I could see better.

We entered the house, and the floors were a beautiful earthy tan and red granite. Some couches and a television were in the living room. Walking through, I saw a dining room with a small standalone sink in the corner. Paintings adorned the walls, and the smell of food permeated the air. I heard my stomach growl and looked down in embarrassment.

Sajith and Sajitha's mother, Sanjana, took my hand and led me to the dining room. She reached for my shoulders and applied a gentle pressure to signal me to sit down. As I sat, she ran to the kitchen. She returned with a glass of water.

After a soft, "Thank you," I drank as I watched her run back to the kitchen.

When she reentered the dining room, she shouted something to the others that prompted them to hurriedly join me at the table. She returned with plates, and I stood to follow her to the kitchen in assistance. With a stern face, she cocked her head sharply to the side, gesturing me to sit down.

After a few minutes, she returned a huge metal bowl of rice.

Everyone scooped it onto their plates.

Lost in my observations, Sajitha scooped for me before I took over the duty.

Their mother returned with another giant metal bowl, this one containing a yellowy liquid I have come to know as *sambhar*. It was like a spicy vegetable soup, and I loved it. The scooping resumed. Now she presented another giant metal bowl containing some sort of vegetable. And then another.

As I scooped, I silently wondered if she was always so prepared. A full meal for five ready in just a few minutes was a pretty big feat, and I aspired to be that level of adult someday. I could barely make myself a sandwich.

I waited to eat until she had taken her seat. As she sat, I lifted my hand to eat, since no spoon was available.

Sanjana jumped from the table and ran again to the kitchen.

What more food can we possibly eat this late at night? I think.

As quickly as she had left, she returned with a spoon in one hand and a fist for the other. I looked at her confusedly, and she patted my head before revealing what she had hidden—a small bar of Dairy Milk.

I might be tired and not at all hungry enough to consume this entire meal, but I could always finish a chocolate bar. Always. When I told her *thank you*, she giggled and then said something to Sajith.

He said to me, "Jurnee Miss, no need for always thank you. It is little funny for us."

I'd tried so many times to stop saying it, but it was such a habit. We continued eating, and I sat in silence as they spoke amongst themselves. I felt left out, but I couldn't blame them. They were a family, and this was their native language. I couldn't help but wonder what my family was doing. They must be awake now; it was Friday afternoon, so they were probably at work. I missed them.

By now, I'd miraculously finished dinner and asked to be excused. I tried to take my plate to the kitchen but was abruptly stopped.

Sanjana took it into the kitchen and pointed to the sink at the side of the room; I was meant to wash up there.

When I turned around, Sajitha had gathered my bag in one hand and took my hand in the other. She led me upstairs and pointed me to which room was hers and where the bathroom was. She also showed me the terrace.

I made an immediate life decision. Wherever I ended up, my future house would have a terrace. I wanted to be close to the stars and looked down over a road. I wanted the treetops to be eye level. Something was so peaceful about being above the hustle and bustle of everyday life.

A young girl living in the neighboring house waved to us from her terrace, and we waved back. Sajitha nodded that we should go inside.

"Which room?" she asked.

All of them seemed fine, but I picked the one with an outlet closest to the bed.

I tossed my bag onto the bed and went into the bathroom to wash my face. I was excited to have a couple days among adults, but the language barrier made me nervous. If only my anxiety was as easy to wash away as the oil on my face.

My phone rang. Anooj. I walked to my room and shut the door before answering. "Hello?"

"*Namaskaram*, Jurnee Miss."

I immediately laughed. "What is this?"

"Nothing, nothing. We just reached home, so I thought to call you."

"How was the journey?"

"Both journey and Jurnee were quite good."

"Ha. Ha." I rolled my eyes. Like I hadn't heard *that* a thousand times in my life.

"I know I told you already, but you wear a saree so beautifully. Even some of the ladies there don't wear it as nicely as you do."

"You know, that it took an actual *team* of three people to do this, right?"

"Of course, but the saree, your hair, the jasmine. You look like a proper *Malayali*."

Unsure of how to reply, I said, "You do too."

He laughed, more than I thought he would. "I'm not a Malayali, Jurnee. My family is from Tamil Nadu, remember. We're only settled in Trivandrum."

"Oh. I'm sorry." I felt like an idiot.

"It's okay. I don't mind. Am I keeping you awake though? I know it's quite late. The kids must be all sleeping nearby."

"No, no. Actually, I'm in the house of one of the students."

"Which?"

"You remember Sajith. The tall boy in tenth. He stays in the hostel."

"Kind of."

"He has glasses."

"Oh, okay."

"I'm staying in his house with his parents and sister."

"Is the house okay? Is the neighborhood safe?"

I said *yes* to everything, and he told me to call him tomorrow if I got time. It was pretty late, and we were both tired. I wanted to chat with someone from home, but everyone always said I should enjoy my surroundings and ignore the internet for some time or that they didn't want to disturb me. But I was bored and wanted to chat.

I reviewed the photos I was tagged in on Facebook and smiled. Today was one of the best days of my life. I plugged in my phone and turned out the light as I contemplated how much I loved it in Kerala and how I truly wished to never leave.

The next morning, I awoke to a knock at the door. Groggily rising from the bed and wiping the black from beneath my eyes, I opened the door. Sanjana. "Good morning, *chechi*," I said to her.

She was noticeably surprised and giggled. "Come," she said with a downward wave of her hand as she turned to walk down the stairs.

I went to wash my face then met her downstairs.

Her husband Suresh was waiting. "Jurnee. Today I show you my store. You meet our family. Some other programs also. Sajith and Sajitha meeting friends."

Their parents were so kind and thoughtful, but I was genuinely worried about spending an entire day with limited communication. The worry subsided when their mom entered the room with a plate of watermelon. She handed me the remote, and their father handed me a newspaper printed in English.

I decided to absentmindedly browse the available channels and eat watermelon. News, soap opera, news, news, Ellen (what?), soap opera, news. Every channel was vastly different, yet one thing remained the same. Each news network had about ten thousand things happening at once. Between the shrill shouting of the several speakers in their individual boxes and the quickly scrolling text, it was almost hypnotic.

Then something incredible happened. The universe conspired in my favor. My jaw dropped in surprise. I involuntarily squealed with joy and immediately recoiled from embarrassment. Here, on a television in a village in India, they were playing *The Lizzie McGuire Movie*—a movie based on my favorite TV show from when I was in eighth grade. English subtitles scrolled below despite the audio being English already, but it wasn't horribly distracting. This is Lizzie McGuire after all, and I will happily endure this small strange inconvenience.

Sanjana sat on the other side of the couch and watched it with me for a few minutes before getting up and walking to the kitchen. She quickly returned with a plate of roasted cashews. They were the most delicious cashews I had ever eaten, and I didn't want them to end. My enthusiasm was interpreted as borderline starvation, and they were quickly refilled.

Jurnee, I angrily thought to myself. *Stop. You'll make their sweet mother do more work if you keep eating like this, not to mention the stomachache waiting for you. Pace yourself, have some self-control.* But I had no self-control. It'd never been my strong suit. If I wanted something, I bought it. If I was hungry, I'd walk to the Domino's across the street and buy a pizza instead of spending a half hour to cook.

Despite my attempts to hide my gluttony, she could sense I wanted more. She returned with more Dairy Milk and said, "*idli*," so at least I'd be consuming something healthy. I wanted to do the polite thing and go into the kitchen after her and offer to help, but, with the language barrier, I was certain I'd only get in her way. She was the nicest person I'd never shared a conversation with.

Before I knew it, Suresh had returned and said we would visit their relatives. He told Sanjana something that prompted her to change into a nicer saree, and we all piled into the car.

I don't know how far we drove or where we were. I had been here for a while, but the views still captivated me—gorgeous trees, people everywhere, the hot sun reaching every corner. Seeing independently run family shops was probably one of my favorite things. No Wal-Marts or Targets, just an unnamed family shop or a Dhanya Supermarket. Walking up to a tiny storefront and reciting a list instead of browsing independently was one of the things that had charmed me the most.

These long, uninterrupted thoughts were very common when I was the lone person in a group who didn't know the language. What could one do without the ability to communicate? Did I make awkward eye contact? No. Play with my phone? A little rude and the battery would drain all too soon. Stare at my shoes and have long talks with myself since no one else would? Yep.

We got to the first relative's house. It was a little smaller than their house but still larger than average. They had ornate wooden chairs with white floral upholstery and a matching couch. A family with two daughters lived here, and I was told they would perform for me. Their father said he had worked in the US before, and his wife smiled. They offered me a variety of cookies and some other snacks while I sat politely on the couch. Sanjana sat beside me and held my hand. At first, it had surprised me, how affectionate people could be, but I'd grown to appreciate it.

The six of us gathered around one of the girls who sat, eyes closed and legs crossed, upon a red blanket on the floor. She sang while slapping her leg to keep the beat. It wasn't a song like I'd heard before though. It was comprised of sudden aspirations. I wasn't sure if it was Malayalam or just sounds, but it hypnotized me. Her face showed such passion as she sang, and I became lost in the beautiful sounds produced from such a small girl.

From nowhere, all the adults recorded me watching her performance. It made the situation that much more awkward, but I was genuinely enjoying it, so at least I didn't have to pretend at all.

When she stopped, I clapped, and, without any break, the other daughter immediately stood ready to dance. She was incredible. Was it common that everyone was good at singing and dancing? Even in the hostel, they were quite gifted.

It reminded me of the dance that the girls in white dresses with decorated hair had performed on Annual Day. The movements were very sharp. She stepped on the floor with such force, and she held such focus that even her fingers and eyes had precise movements. In awe of her concentration, I realized my mouth was agape, and I had completely forgotten about the cameras and the entire room watching me.

"Good?" their father asked with a shake of his head.

I smiled and nodded with an, "Excellent!"

The family stood to take selfies with us, and then we piled into the car to return home.

I didn't understand anything they said on the way home, but everything looked so beautiful in the moonlight. *There's nothing like this back home*, I couldn't help but to think to myself. *I never want to leave.* I could probably learn Malayalam; it couldn't be that difficult. I could probably even get a visa and maybe stay permanently in the hostel.

When we reached the house, I realized it was past eleven, so I told everyone goodnight and began to head upstairs.

"No!" they both called at one.

I eyed Sanjana, and she gestured toward the kitchen. I couldn't possibly eat more after the snacks we'd had at their relative's house, but saying *no* was so difficult.

We entered the kitchen, and she pulled some metal pots and their covers from a cupboard. It was food from earlier today. She ran back into the kitchen, and I sat with Suresh.

"You like dancing, singing?" he asked me.

"Yes, Uncle. They were very good."

"You want to learn?"

If only he knew how little rhythm I had, he would not have asked this question. "No, sir. I cannot."

"Any religion problem?"

I was briefly confused before remembering that some specific groups of Christians here didn't dance. "No, I just don't know how."

"You will learn. Do not worry."

I smiled. I never realized it was possible for anyone to be so kind to me, especially someone I barely knew.

Sanjana returned with the *idlis*. I tried to serve myself, but she wouldn't allow it. She and Suresh chatted in Malayalam, so I ate quietly.

I wondered what my family was doing, my friends, my students, Anooj. Had I missed anything interesting at home? Could I find a job when I got back? I wished I could use my phone, but I didn't want to seem rude at the dinner table when everyone had been so kind to me.

Sanjana stood and came to collect my plate.

I had always tried to silently tell her I was capable of taking my dishes to wash, but she won every time. It didn't seem fair she would do all the cooking and all the cleaning, but Suresh interrupted my internal debate. "You are the guest, Jurnee. Relax."

I smiled and look down, but a deafening sound interrupted me. It was like a marching band had spontaneously appeared in front of the house.

Suresh saw my confusion. "Procession. Come and see."

The three of us went out together and marveled at the lit floats and tiny parade crossing through the middle of the night. Everyone was outside for the parade. I didn't realize so many Christians lived here.

"They're all Christians?" I asked him.

"No. We are Hindu. They are Hindu. They are Hindu. They are Muslim." He pointed out the neighboring houses. "Christian enjoy Muslim festival. Hindu enjoy Christian festival. Muslim enjoy Hindu festival. All respect others."

It was a nice sentiment. Every place should strive to achieve such harmony between religions.

We stood for a bit longer before he said, "You must feel tired. Go and sleep."

I *was* tired, but I had also been nervous to say I wanted to go to bed for fear of seeming rude.

I walked through the living room and up the now familiar staircase. Once out of view, I removed my phone and walked onto the terrace. The air was so fresh, so warm. Trees grew in every direction, and I had never felt so surrounded by nature. Some were tall, some short, some with giant leaves, some with small leaves. I wondered why so many people dreamed of living abroad when they had been born into a paradise.

I tried to take a picture, but the quality in the dark wasn't very good, so I made note to take one with the sunrise. If I could stay here forever, it wouldn't be long enough. After one last glance around, I went inside to sleep.

The next morning, I'd missed the sunrise but immediately ran to the terrace to take a photo. I posted it to Facebook as I walked to the bathroom to get ready for the day. Now that I'd learned how showers work, life was much easier.

I checked in again with my parents and saw Anooj's message. I had totally forgotten I was supposed to call him earlier.

Ring ring. Ring ring.

"I thought you were going to call yesterday. I was worried."

"Why?"

"You're staying in someone's house. How do you know it's safe?"

"It's my student's family." What did I possibly have to worry about? I even ran it by Joseph to make sure it was fine.

"Can I talk to them?"

"No."

"I just want to check something. Please?"

With a sigh, I surrendered and walked downstairs, phone in hand. I saw the table littered with bowls of food ready for all of us.

"Today, I will show you the land," Suresh announced.

"Actually, my friend wants to speak with you really quick," I said nervously.

He took the phone and introduced himself. "I am Suresh."

When I heard the faint sound of Anooj switching to Malayalam, I saw his face change. He was happily surprised, and, after a few minutes, he returned my phone. "Nice boy."

"Any problem?" Why had Anooj insisted on speaking with him?

"All fine."

I was shocked that he cared this much to take the time to speak with Sajith's father. I looked down to conceal my smile.

We sat across from each other at the dining room table as steam billowed from the various bowls. Sanjana was making fresh *dosas*, and the smell was the most majestic, heavenly scent I had ever encountered. I wanted so badly to copy some recipes, but I thought it wouldn't be possible due to the language barrier.

I ate quickly—but not too quickly so as not to accidentally show I was famished. In reality, I just really wanted to go on the tour.

She had perfectly prepared and beautifully displayed each dish with garnishments. It must have taken her ages to make such a feast, and she did it multiple times per day. She must work harder than anyone, with all the effort that goes into making these dishes. It was like Thanksgiving every day.

They chatted in Malayalam as I scanned the room. I thought about how much I'd miss them but dismissed it and forced myself to live in the moment and enjoy the time we were together now.

Suresh stood and called me to join him. I looked to Sanjana, silently asking if she needed my help to clear the table, but she smiled and nodded, telling me to go. We'd nearly mastered this silent communication.

We walked to the front door and put on our shoes. It still shocked me that everyone here wore flip-flops almost exclusively, and also that I was now one of them. It was just so much more convenient since we had to remove our shoes fairly often. Turning right, we passed the trees beside the house and entered into the backyard. Tall, thin trees sprawled as far as the eye could see, towering over all the other trees, and had small green hoods around them with a dark black line.

He noted my confusion. "Rubber trees." He then brought me to a small workshop with a machine that has two long rollers and a handle. With a quick demonstration, he turned a bit of fresh black rubber goop into a sheet. It was clear it took considerable strength.

Wait. This was where rubber comes from? I always knew it came from trees, and I had read that Kerala produced the majority of Indian rubber during my research; I just thought that they would be bigger. They were so thin and so tall. I couldn't believe it.

We walked through the back yard for several minutes through several perfect rows of trees. They were beautiful, and I never realized how nature provided us with so much more than food. This really is *God's Own Country*.

There were birds, some flies, and a few chipmunks. There were so many trees and no evidence of humans, apart from the fact that we were standing there. It was an enchanting sight, the epitome of tranquility. We finally returned to the house.

"How is it?" Suresh asked.

"Beautiful, Uncle."

The sun pouring through the endless rows of trees didn't even look real. Sure, it was sweltering hot even in February, but I couldn't get the thought from my mind that I belonged here, that I never wanted to leave.

Reaching the back of the house, I saw a wider variety of trees.

He showed me a short, wide, and dense tree. "Mango tree." He taught me to identify it by the long, shiny green leaves. He showed me a baby mango and cut it down. He shouted something to Sanjana, and she quickly came out holding a small metal plate with a red powder and white granules. "Try this," he said as he cut slits in the mango. "Mango with salt and chili powder."

Sanjana stood waiting while mixing the two into one.

That sounded absolutely awful, but who was I to say *no* to trying new things? "Wow!" was the only thing I could think to say.

Sanjana smiled the most innocent and genuine smile I had ever seen as she sprinkled the mixture into the slits.

I was extremely nervous and hoped one of them would eat it first as a quick tutorial, so I didn't look weird if I did it wrong, but they gave it to me first. Nervously, I took the mango and gingerly bit into it and was pleasantly surprised. Despite the bizarre mixture of flavors, it was actually delicious.

They immediately looked for more mangos to cut down. Sanjana and Suresh were so sweet, but they were doing too much work for me.

I felt so guilty with how kind they were and how much effort they put into my stay. "No, no. It's okay," I said to stop them.

"Okay then, next you see jackfruit tree."

We came upon a normal-looking tree with smooth bark, but giant green bulbous things emerged from the trunk. Their lumps almost looked as if it had some kind of fungus. I remembered seeing one of these in the school grounds also. Was this what it had been?

He climbed the tree with a knife and a rope in hand.

I was momentarily worried until I remembered he must do this all the time, so it was probably not a big deal.

When he reached the green bulbous part, he tied the rope around it and cut the stem. He effortlessly but carefully lowered it to the ground with the rope, so I decided to do my part and carry it inside. But I couldn't lift it, I could barely roll it. He laughed. "Heavy, *aa*?"

"Yes, very heavy."

He picked up the jackfruit as if it was a shoe, without any hesitation or struggle. "Sanjana!" he called as he carried it inside.

I stood, taking in the numerous varieties of trees surrounding me. At least a half dozen more trees must have been just in this tiny part of the yard. How was that possible? I could at least recognize the banana trees from the hostel; though I still found it strange the bananas grew upside down. They looked so heavy, like the branch may snap under the weight.

"She will cut," he said as he came back outside to continue the tour.

"Great!" I was so curious to see what was growing inside the giant bulbous pod as I followed him to the banana tree I had just spotted.

He pulled a banana from the giant clump.

"No, really. I've eaten too much today."

"Jurnee, you are our guest. We will show you our Kerala."

Who can say *no* to that? I don't even like bananas, but I don't want to disappoint him.

He plucked it and even peeled it before handing it to me.

It was surprisingly tasty. I couldn't even stand the smell of bananas back home, and I wanted to ask him why this one tasted so much better, but he hadn't been to the US to try our bananas, so he wouldn't know. I was really feeling full now though. *I can't possibly eat anymore*, I thought as Sanjana emerged from the house with a plate of jackfruit. Ohh! I *have* had these before. They were sweet fleshy bits often made into a curry—fried or eaten raw. Ajitha Miss often brought some to school for me. I didn't know they grew inside that giant fruit though. I was constantly in awe of nature while I was here. This was the coolest thing.

I took just one piece. I was feeling really sick now and didn't want to take too much. I was careful to eat it very slowly, so no one mistakenly thought I was starving and tried to get me to eat more. It tasted so fresh and perfect, and I wanted more, but I couldn't possibly.

Suresh insisted I have another, but I politely declined. Between the heat and how full I had become, it was a very bad idea. I wanted to go inside but there were still a few trees left to explore, and I loved this tour.

He showed me some of the *chambakka* trees just like the ones by the doors of the hostel. The tiny immaculate fruits were like picture perfect little pink bells. Luckily, he accepted my excuse that I was full, and we moved on. He showed me cashews growing, seemingly hanging from apples. Each fruit grew just one nut, and I now understand why cashews were so expensive. He showed me peppercorns growing on the trunk of a tree, green and round until they turned black after drying in the sun.

I marveled at every small detail.

We continued to another tree. This one looked strange; long sticks sprouted straight out at the top. I'd not seen anything even remotely like it before, and I was curious to see what it was, but I knew that would mean I'd have to eat and I couldn't possibly eat even a little bit more.

"Papaya!" Suresh exclaimed as he cut off a fruit.

I weakly smiled. I would happily try it with dinner, but I'd already eaten so much today. One person was not possibly meant to consume this much food in a single day, let alone in half a day. "Can we eat it with dinner?"

"No. Right now only is fresh. Eat."

"I've eaten too much. I'll vomit." I hold my stomach for dramatic effect.

"That is no problem, Jurnee. We have a lot of land. Go and vomit behind that tree and come."

I stopped. Was he serious? He had said it completely un-ironically. He actually wanted me to vomit, then return and eat a fresh papaya. There was no way. "Please. I'm feeling very sick."

"Okay *molu*."

I immediately felt awful. Here he was, so excited for me to try the fruits, and he looked so defeated now. I literally couldn't eat another bite though, but I had to do something.

"One piece only. We'll have balance with dinner." I hated saying *balance*, but I had learned at the hostel everyone thought I was talking about sleeping rest whenever I said *the rest*. I hoped this would make it up to him a little bit, and it worked.

He smiled and cut a piece about a cubic inch in size.

"It's so good, Uncle. Very fresh."

His smile grew even more. "Now go and take rest before dinner."

I couldn't possibly imagine eating another meal right now and briefly wondered how much weight I had gained just in these past few days. "Okay, sure. Thank you for the fruit and the tour."

"Don't want to keep telling *thank you, thank* you for everything."

I didn't know what to say, so I smiled and walked into the house.

Sanjana and I greeted each other with a smile, and I gestured to say that I was going upstairs.

She responded with a motion imitating sleep, and I nodded to confirm.

When I got upstairs, I checked my phone to see what I had missed. Facebook revealed a friend's engagement party. I felt so disconnected from everyone while being away, but I decided to see the photos later. I sent my parents a quick check-in text and a short greeting to Anooj before resuming my scrolling through Facebook to see what else I had missed.

My phone rang. Anooj.

"Hello?" I said quietly so no one would realize I wasn't asleep.

"What happened? Why so quiet?"

"I'm supposed to be taking a nap," I said in hushed tones as I explained my morning to him.

He teased me for how excited I was about having seen how they made rubber but was happy to hear I had liked all the fruit.

We talked for a bit longer, but soon my exhaustion won over, and I fell asleep during the call.

CHAPTER 9

Sitting with Suresh on the front porch, he began a casual interrogation. "Jurnee, you are married?"

"No."

"Your marriage is fixed?"

I paused for a moment. Fixed? Ohh, yes. Fixed, like set. "No."

"Your parents are looking for a boy?"

Now was hardly the time to discuss cultural differences, so I played along. "Not yet, Uncle."

He became silent, but his face grew serious.

Unsure of where to look, I stared at my feet.

"Tonight, we go to temple," he said after a long, uncomfortable pause.

I had really wanted to see one, but why *now*? Was I getting married tonight? Did Hindus get married in temples, as we marry in churches? One of my Hindu friends back home had gotten married in a hotel, but, then again, I have Christian friends who got married in hotels also. In a silent yet panicked prayer, I asked God to allow me to go home unmarried.

Suresh stood and went inside.

The warm breeze whistled through the trees, and I opened my phone to consult Anooj. *Busy?* I sent the quick message then closed WhatsApp and browsed Facebook for a couple of minutes.

What happened?

Apparently, I'm going to a temple tonight. Why? What do I wear? Is it possible to accidentally get married?

What? he typed, followed by several laughing emojis.

I narrated the entire conversation to him, body language and inflections included, and waited anxiously for a response.

Ayy, Jurnee. Relax. There is a small belief here that if a girl is unmarried past 23 years that maybe she will not get a quality husband. They just want to take you to perform a small ritual as a prayer for your God to grant you a nice husband.

That was certainly a relief, but one problem remained. *What do I wear though????*

Sanjana Auntie will help you. Don't take tension.

Of course. Why do I overthink everything? *You're a lifesaver,* I messaged.

Besides this, are you ok? Is the food still fine?

Ya, all is fine. What about you?

I am fine. Just on break from working.

Ok, carry on, I wrote as I closed out of WhatsApp.

A notification popped up. *Call me if any problems.*

I laughed quietly to myself, thinking that Anooj must be my guardian angel in India. Anytime I needed food, help, or a cultural explanation, he was right there.

The afternoon passed slowly as Sanjana and I watched soap opera after soap opera while eating my new favorite snack, Kerala Mixture. I had no idea what the characters were saying or what was happening, but their expressions were incredibly dramatic, and the camera seemed to pan to each one after every line of dialogue. It was addictive.

After some time, she motioned to the upstairs, and I followed her into my room. She opened my suitcase and rummaged through my potential outfits for the temple. Jeans rejected; long skirt rejected. I was surprised she also rejected my *saree* from Annual Day. A nod of approval came at the sight of my simple black leggings as she sat them aside with a long fitted shirt and its matching scarf.

I accepted her decision and put them on as she smiled and rubbed my arm. A pang of sadness came suddenly that we could never keep in touch due to language barriers, but I pushed it away. I scolded myself, *Now is hardly the time to get sentimental.*

Sanjana stood and gestured for me to follow. We went downstairs—her in front and me close behind, like a dog or baby duck—around the corner and into her room. She pressed her hands on my arms.

I sat obediently and waited as she left and returned with a comb. Sitting on the bed with her combing my hair behind me took me back to Ananya when she had styled my hair for Annual Day. She pulled back two small pieces of hair from each side and braided them together where they met in the back, just as Ananya had. She was so gentle and kind.

As she walked around to the front, she smiled and opened a box on the table. Earrings. So many earrings. After much deliberation, she decided on some small gold ones that bore a slight resemblance to a bottomless birdcage. She put them in my ears and uttered a single word, "*Sundhari*"—Malayalam for *beautiful*.

I smiled at her, and she took my hand, leading me to the living room.

Suresh and a girl about my age were waiting.

Sanjana nudged me to go with them.

Was she not coming? I hesitantly eyed the girl, and she told me to come as she took my hand.

The three of us piled into the car and drove for what seemed like hours. It was probably fifteen minutes; my anxiety just hates me. When we reached the temple, I was slightly underwhelmed. I had been expecting a large, grand building with a big crowd, but it was just a couple of small structures and a handful of people.

As we got out of the car, every eye was on me—all six of them. I looked at my feet and followed the girl toward the main area. It didn't seem that she knew English, so we communicated largely with a makeshift sign language, similar to how I communicated with Sanjana.

Tube lights were nestled into the tree branches, and each structure had doors, a god, and a short but wide oil lamp. The priest was surprisingly young and wore a simple *mundu* with a string around his torso, and three white lines painted horizontally on his forehead. He approached us, and the girl handed him a small amount of money.

Together she and I stood in silence a few feet in front of the main structure. I watched as he lit the lamp and chanted. He sprinkled a liquid and then flower petals. I wanted to ask what was happening and the meanings behind the different actions, but I didn't want to interrupt and miss something. He smeared something onto a leaf. Then he put ashes on it. This leaf was then transferred into a plastic bag and given to me.

Suresh came to collect us. I thanked the priest, and we headed to the car. Inspecting the leaf in the bag, my curiosity was exploding as three boys walking arm in arm passed us on their way to the temple. The middle one peered at me and smiled, but I looked down to avoid prolonged eye contact as I'd been told it may accidentally convey interest.

In the car, Suresh announced, "Jurnee, now you will find a husband within six months."

I wasn't sure what a good response to that would be, so I smiled to him as I texted Anooj. *Guess who got a magic husband leaf.*

A what?

A magic husband leaf.

So, you married a magic leaf, or this leaf will find a husband for you?

It'll find a husband for me. I hope I get a human husband and not a leaf husband by mistake.

Show me the leaf.

In the car now. I'll send it when we get home.

Ok sure. I take it you didn't get married then?

Not yet. I'm safe for now. I added a tongue emoji.

Leaning my head against the window, I looked upon the village. As much fun as I was having, I couldn't help but miss the kids at the hostel and wonder if they missed me too. They must be getting ready for bed now.

Before I knew it, we had reached the house, and I carried my magic husband leaf inside.

Suresh beamed with pride. "Your arms look like tube lights."

I turned to smile, unsure if this was a compliment, just as Sanjana stopped me and asked, via charades, if I was hungry. "No, no." I put my hand on my stomach and hoped this would convey how full I was.

She still ran to the kitchen and returned with two plain *idli*.

I couldn't help but think how much weight I would gain if I lived in this house full time. I took my *idlis* upstairs and ate them while catching up on Facebook and text messages. Then the most annoying part of life happened; I finally got ready for bed and realized I wasn't tired anymore.

Not wanting to call internationally or disturb anyone while they were at work or in class, I called Anooj. I hoped he wouldn't be too annoyed by me calling him just after we had texted.

"Not having dinner?" Anooj asked, concerned, instead of greeting me.

"I'm not hungry but was still forced to take *idli*. I've never eaten this much in my life," I said, chuckling.

"She only wants you to be well fed and have a proper Kerala experience."

"I know, but no one back home will recognize me if I continue eating this much."

He laughed heartily then halted. "Jurnee?"

"What's up?"

"I'm really glad that I was your driver that day."

"Me too. But enough about me, what have you been up to all day?"

"Not much. Just went to the office and watched TV. An average day. I'm still waiting for that photo, by the way."

"Oh! I completely forgot. One second." I quickly took the photo and sent it via WhatsApp.

"Wow. Definitely you'll get a quality husband with this leaf."

"You can't be serious," I said in a doubtful tone while simultaneously wondering if he was actually serious.

"I honestly don't even know what ritual this is that they did," he said, laughing. "You foreigners are so gullible."

"I'm deeply offended. Goodnight!" I said sarcastically.

But he didn't catch on. "*Ayyy* no, Jurnee. Sorry, *da*. Please don't be upset."

"Now who's the gullible one, eh?"

We both laughed.

I heard footsteps running up the stairs and coming closer then a knock on the door.

"Jurnee?" Suresh asked.

"Yes, sir?"

"All okay?"

"Sorry. Just call with friends. I'll sleep now."

"Goodnight, dear."

I wished him goodnight, and I heard the footsteps resume, then they became fainter with each step.

"I guess we'd better sleep," I said to Anooj.

"Goodnight, *yathra*."

"What's that?"

"The Malayalam word for *journey*."

I wished I knew a cool language to reciprocate the sentiment, but I only know English, so all I could say was *goodnight*.

I was supposed to be back at school by now, but I decided one more day wouldn't hurt.

Sajitha and Sajith had been spending time with their friends, and, now home, their father took the morning to drive them to their schools

As Sanjana and I watched TV together, she motioned me to the spare room on the ground floor.

I obediently stood to follow her.

She pressed my shoulder to ask me to sit as she walked behind me, comb in hand. It was times like these I would really like to speak with her. I was sure she was as nice in speaking as she was in behavior, but I'll never know. She braided my hair as she sang. I didn't understand a word, but it was beautiful. She continued as she straightened my shirt and silently nodded in approval.

Suresh arrived and said it was time to go.

"Where are we going?" Probably to another relative's house, but one can never be sure.

"Relative's house," he confirmed.

Sanjana took her cute, small bag, and we all together got into the car. They talked, but I didn't understand a word. I really wished that I knew Malayalam.

The house before us was moderately large, and a beautiful bright blue. We got out of the car and I walked behind them as we removed our shoes. They knocked on the door and I continued standing behind them while we waited.

They exchanged excited pleasantries with a middle-aged lady. She invited us inside, and I heard *chaiyya*, so definitely tea was in the near future. They talked as she silently directed me to sit on the couch. Only a moment later, they'd left me alone.

I was used to being isolated in conversations, but actually being left alone in a stranger's house without even an introduction was uncomfortable. I felt a bit annoyed, but the tea was so good that I couldn't stay angry.

An older lady briefly peeked through the doorway, and I waved invitingly. Even if we didn't speak, some company was better than none. She declined my offer and walked away. Had I done something wrong?

An oddly familiar-looking man entered the room. "Jurnee Miss?"

"Do I know you?"

"I am Aneesh."

Oh! He was the guy at the temple in the group who were arriving as we were leaving, the one who looked at me.

"From the temple!"

"So, you do remember me," he said with a smile as he revealed he had brought cookies for the tea. "Biscuit?"

In this moment, I was torn. On one side, I was so excited to speak proper English and have cookies, but, on the other side, I knew it was improper for a girl to talk to a boy, and enough stereotypes existed here about foreigners that I certainly didn't want to add to them.

I nodded in an attempt to be polite yet short to avoid anyone thinking negatively and grabbed a cookie.

"So, what brought you to Kerala?"

"I'm teaching at a nearby school."

"St. Joseph's, right?"

"Yes."

"And you're teaching English?"

"How do you know this?"

"I teach science nearby."

I silently wondered if a secret network of locals who gossip about foreigners existed. "Cool."

"What classes English do you teach?"

"LKG through eighth. They say the older kids need to focus more on their exams."

"Yes, correct. The tenth standard board exam is very important, you know."

"I've heard, yes."

"So, what do you do in America?"

"I just graduated with my elementary education degree, and I'm searching for a job."

"Great! Are you enjoying Kerala?"

"It's really nice. I've made some great friends, and it's so beautiful."

"Do you think you could live in Kerala?"

"I heard a Domino's is opening nearby, so probably," I joked.

He laughed. Someone here in the village laughed at a joke I made. I was so relieved. "Very funny, Jurnee Miss. Have you learned to cook Kerala food?"

"Just *Jurnee* is fine, no need to be formal."

He nodded politely then gestured with his hand that I should continue answering.

My mind recalled Anooj and how he had teased me with *Just Jurnee* when we first met. "I've seen Cook Auntie making food, but I haven't learned much myself, as there's such a language barrier."

"Don't worry. My mother will teach you. Actually, I saw a photo of you in a *saree*. Did you learn yourself to drape it, or did you need help?"

These questions were getting awfully personal. Was this normal? I assumed he was just curious about foreigners and continued the interrogation game. "It took a team of three teachers, actually." I laughed.

He didn't join me in my laughter this time. "You will learn in time. Don't worry. My mother will be happy to teach you that also."

Why was his mother suddenly my mentor? I smiled politely to not show too much confusion.

"Do you use the Facebook?"

I felt like I'd added half the village to my Facebook, so I couldn't possibly lie and say *no*. I nodded, and he asked me to find my profile in the app on his phone.

We officially became *friends*, and he smiled as he scrolled through my photos *right in front of me*.

"You know … we are renovating the entire upstairs to be a suite for me and my wife after marriage."

"Oh, congratulations!" I didn't know he was engaged. I shouldn't have misinterpreted the exchange as weird flirting. I immediately let down my guard and relaxed as I finished another cookie.

"No, no. We didn't yet find a girl."

"*We?*"

"My mother and I."

"Your mother will marry the girl too?" I know that wasn't how it worked, but it sounded odd.

"No, Jurnee dear. We didn't yet find a girl for me to marry. None are as good as you."

Oh, no. This was going where I thought it was going. I smiled, mouth closed, and looked to the side to try to find Sajith's parents. I needed them to rescue me.

"Jurnee?"

"What's up?"

"Would you like to make my mother your mother-in-law?"

Holy Baby Jesus. Was this a proposal? What was this? What was happening? What were the consequences if I declined? Would Sajith's parents look bad? Was this planned?

I was so confused, but, with some quick thinking, I rebutted, "I really shouldn't make such a big decision without my parents." Respectable yet vague, perfect.

He beamed. "I never imagine a foreign girl will care about the opinion of her family. You really are like us, dear."

Finally, Sajith's parents reappeared. Maybe this *was* planned after all. They hugged and bid farewell as the three of us returned to the car.

"Do you like Aneesh?" Suresh didn't wait for even a second.

"He's okay." I didn't want to be rude, but I didn't want to pretend to be interested. Then it hit me. Was this the work of the magic husband leaf?

CHAPTER 10

As we approached the school's gate, I felt guilty for feeling so happy. I had loved spending time with Sajith's family, but I really missed the hustle and bustle of being around everyone. Since it was midday, they were all in school, but I'd join them later. The security guard allowed us to pass, and we drove to the basketball court. I hugged Sanjana and waved to Suresh as I took my bag and walked down the steps to the hostel.

The dogs were out of the cages, which was odd, but I didn't think anything of it and continued to the front door. It was locked. Of course, it was locked. I walked around the side to the kitchen door. Crossing the trees and row of sinks, I prayed it would be open, because, if it wasn't, I'd have no other choice but to stay outside or go to school carrying all my things. It was closed. I knocked softly at first then progressively louder. After a couple of minutes, Cook Auntie came to rescue me.

She beamed and gestured that I should wait a moment, so I sat on the plastic chair as she made me a cup of tea. I never knew, before coming to India, that it was possible to be so close to someone without speaking a word to each other.

She handed me the metal cup, and I gestured that she should also have some. She declined at first but accepted after some prodding.

We entered the study hall room and drank our tea in a comfortable silence.

I smiled at her and nodded to the door, as though asking permission to go, and she wiggled her head with approval. I quickly washed my glass and went upstairs to put away my things before I headed to school. Only a couple of hours were left, but I might as well be somewhat useful.

I tried to shower due to standing outside in the heat, but I had forgotten they regularly shut off the water in the mornings for conservation so I'd have to wait until evening. I took the time to unpack my things instead.

I grabbed my notebook and decided to donate one of my books to the library. I hurriedly locked the door and headed downstairs. I couldn't go through the front door since it was locked, so I crossed through the kitchen again and waved goodbye to Cook Auntie.

One of the dogs ran up to me, and I took a moment to pet her. I thought it was Jimikki. She was so soft one with white spots on the back of her ears, like earrings. I scratched her behind her ears, and she closed her eyes in ecstasy. I loved these dogs so much. Well, really any dog, but I quite liked this batch. I rose to walk down the path to school, and she followed me. "Jimikki," I said in a commanding voice. "Stay." I knew she didn't understand, but did any dog *really* know English? Especially one from Kerala?

Much to my surprise, she sat. I turned slowly and proceeded to school. It didn't take long, however, to realize she had resumed following me.

"Jimikki. No!"

She cocked her head in confusion and didn't even pretend to sit. She'd follow me into school, I just knew it.

"Jimikki. Really. Please stay. I don't think you're allowed to come to school." Pleading with her as though she could understand would work, right? It worked in movies where dogs could magically understand and save the day; why couldn't she magically understand and stay outside?

I was almost under the awning, and so was she. "Okay, you win," I said as we went through the back door.

Everyone was in their classroom at first, so no one took notice to Jimikki following me, as if I were her mother duck. It didn't take long for bored, mid-afternoon students gazing out their classroom windows to notice a dog on the premises though. Before I knew it, kids had crowded around the windows, and a couple teachers had taken notice.

One who had come out before realizing Jimikki was loose was noticeably frightened. She called across the courtyard to ask if I was okay, and I replied that I was fine. It was quite impressive how well Jimikki followed me. In that moment, I wanted more than anything to bring her home with me.

When I reached the office, Nissy saw me and welcomed me back. And then she noticed the dog. She expressed concern over Jimikki's presence, and I immediately apologized. I explained what had happened, and her concern changed to being impressed.

"Have you trained her in any other tricks?" she asked.

"No, but I definitely think she's capable."

"I do too. Suggest it to Joseph Sir that we teach her something useful. But in the meantime, it may be best to take her outside."

"Okay, I'll just be back." I set my things on the ground and turned to Jimikki. As I lifted her like a baby, I heard roaring laughter come from some of the classrooms. Jimikki and I headed outside, and I locked her into her crate. "Bye, little one. We'll see you in a couple hours." I reached my hand through the bars of the door to pet her. She wasn't at all little, but I loved her. "Be good," I finished with one last scratch on her head.

Walking back to the school, I was so excited to see everyone again, until a girl in ninth approached, giggling and covering her mouth. "Jurnee Miss! You have become so fat in only one weekend! How?"

I felt my face redden. Was she serious? I knew people spoke more bluntly here, but that was just rude. I smiled politely and continued walking but was stopped dead in my tracks.

"You're just jealous that she had lots of tasty food because your mother is bad in cooking!" I was blessed by the arrival of one of my fifth-grade friends. "Come, Jurnee Miss, my class is so much missing you." She took my hand and ran down the hallway.

The rest of the school day was filled with announcements of my weight gain and declarations of missingness.

At dinner with the fifth-grade boys, Sachin declared, "Jurnee Miss, you shouldn't leave."

The others immediately chimed in.

"Who will get me a visa then?" I asked.

A few offered to ask their parents for help, and I genuinely contemplated it, but I had to eventually go back. As much as I loved the people, and as much fun as I was having, it wasn't home. There was a language barrier, the food was different, I was away from my friends and family. I would do anything to stay, but it just wasn't realistic. I was amused for a moment about how reluctant I had been to expand my job search to one hundred miles back home, but now I was seriously considering moving ten thousand miles away.

"Jurnee Miss …" Joseph startled me when he suddenly approached the table.

"Yes, sir?"

"From tomorrow, please sit with Nelson and Krishna during study hall. They need to practice their reading and focus on their studies. Kids here are great at recitation, but we want to encourage critical thinking and making sure they really understand. Learning is about more than just memorization."

"Okay, sir." I tried not to sound too excited. I loved Nelson and Krishna. Well, I loved all of them, but I was ecstatic to be forced to hang out with them. I mean, *to help them study.*

The next evening, we were sitting outside on the steps after school while the boys put on their soccer shoes for sports period.

"Jurnee Miss, the coconuts are so looking so good."

I looked up. What was the difference between a good and bad coconut? They all appeared the same. "Yeah, really nice ones!"

"At my home, I always have coconut water."

"That's so cool. How do you get to it?"

"Have you not seen someone getting a coconut before?"

Should I have? Was this common knowledge? Embarrassed, I admitted that, indeed, I had not ever seen someone harvest a coconut. I'd eaten lots of fresh fruit at Sajith's house, but I didn't get to watch them cut down the coconut. *Cut down? Harvested? Acquired?* I had no idea of the correct terminology.

I noticed, from the corner of my eye, one of the bus drivers watching us curiously. When he approached, I realized it was Nehemiah. I really liked Nehemiah. He was so nice, and the kids really seemed to like him. He had even brought me a small chocolate bar once. I think it had been Dairy Milk. I really didn't understand the name though. Dairy and milk were made redundant. And they also indicated liquid. But it was solid chocolate. Puzzling, yet delicious.

Nehemiah said something to me in Malayalam and snapped me from my thoughts. I didn't know why some people spoke to me in Malayalam, but I didn't say anything. I felt like he was asking a question by his tone, so I shrugged.

Nasim, my favorite third grader on this earth, decided to be my interpreter. "Jurnee Miss, Nehemiah Uncle says that it is very bad that you haven't had fresh coconut water with us before."

How should one respond to that? Confused, I shrugged again. "Sorry, *da*." I laughed at myself. I was like a friend's mom who tried to use the current slang but just sounds stupid. My suspicions were proven correct when they began to giggle. Yep, I was the weird old lady.

Before I could blame myself for upsetting him, I noticed him get into the school bus, park it beneath one of the coconut trees, and begin to climb it. I stared in awe, wishing that I could climb giant things. I looked from student to student to check if they were seeing this also or if I was imagining it. "Is he going to climb the tree?"

"Of course, Jurnee Miss. We want you to have coconut water with us."

"But how will he climb such a thin tree? There are no branches to hold."

"See the cuts in the wood, *na*? He will use those."

I looked closely and, sure enough, slivers of the tree were cut out. I still watched in amazement. One day, I hoped to have enough upper body strength to climb a coconut tree. Or a school bus. Even a short fence.

"But how will he get down? Is it safe? Should we help him?"

"No, no. Jurnee Miss, don't worry so much. We are Malayalis." He flexed his tiny third-grade biceps.

In the moment I had looked away, Nehemiah had jumped to the school bus. I briefly wondered from what height he had jumped, if he was okay, how long he'd been climbing trees, and how he'd learned. But I didn't want to act like an idiot foreigner amazed by every small thing and turn a common activity into an interrogation.

I did notice, however, that he had thrown the coconut to the ground. That definitely made sense, because it would be quite cumbersome to carry down a coconut.

He jumped from the bus, grabbed the coconut and ran to the steps. Nehemiah pointed to the tree, looked at me and shook his head, as if to ask if I had seen.

I nodded and added, "Super."

He smiled and shut his eyes briefly before pointing to the side of the hostel with the kitchen entrance and nodding.

I looked at Nasim, knower of all things, for guidance.

"Jurnee Miss, he will go to get a knife now."

I nodded and smiled.

Nehemiah quickly returned with glasses and a thick, curved knife.

I checked to see if Cook Auntie had also come, but she must be busy.

He cut the coconut in one swift motion and poured the liquid between the glasses.

I was surprised no one had noticed we weren't at sports time, but I excitedly grabbed a glass with the others. We clinked for cheers, but no one drank.

"Jurnee Miss, you must first drink."

I lifted my glass, as if to toast, and sipped. It was so fresh, like drinking sunshine.

They approved of my reaction and drank from their glasses as well.

I entered the study hall room and noticed Nelson and Krishna at their regular table in the corner. "Nelson. Krishna."

"Jurnee Miss."

It all felt so formal, and they looked confused at how seriously and frankly I had addressed them. "Come with me. Bring your things."

"Miss. Any problem?" Krishna asked, concerned.

I had to try hard to maintain my serious composure. "You'll see."

They glanced at each other, both slightly worried, as we walked out of the study hall room, past the foyer, and to the front steps.

I sat on the steps and gestured for them to join me. "We'll study out here from now on."

"Just the three of us?" Nelson asked.

"Yes. MD Sir has asked that I help both of you with your reading, so let's get started. Where are you in your book?"

Krishna took his book and pointed to the page.

I glanced through it to get an idea of what the material was and then asked him to read it.

He read slowly from *The Bazaars of Hyderabad*, struggling over some of the words, but he could get through most of it.

I turned to Nelson. "Please continue the passage."

He struggled a little bit as well, but it was clear it was more of a confidence issue than a language issue.

"You both are doing a great job, just a couple things we may want to work on."

I noticed them tense up. It was my job to inspire them to enjoy reading and not to be ashamed or embarrassed by it.

"Let's try this. I'll read the next passage, and you both imitate me." Maybe that would help take the pressure off them to build their confidence a bit more. It had just the reverse effect. They looked bored out of their minds. "Jurnee Miss, do we really have to do this?"

"It was MD Sir's request. Let's try something else though."

They immediately looked relieved. This must be absolute torture, being singled out like this. I needed to make it fun. "Let's act it out!"

They again glanced at each other worriedly.

"It'll be fun. Come on, just try one part."

Nelson shrugged with a wiggle of his head to confirm he would try, and this left Krishna with no choice but to comply.

"I'll go first." The passage mentioned fruits, so I grabbed Krishna's backpack and cradled it like a fruit basket, pretending to be a vendor as I held the invisible fruits before their eyes.

"Jurnee Miss, you look like a mental," they said, laughing almost in unison. At least I was making it memorable though; there was a method to my madness.

"Maybe I am, but one of you will be next. Who wants to be a musician?"

Krishna meekly raised his hand. The passage spoke of instruments, and he banged an invisible drum as I overenthusiastically yet silently applauded and whistled.

I might be making a fool of myself to a pair of sixth graders, but at least they were learning. "You're up next, Nelson!"

He looked around nervously to ensure no one else could see what he was about to do. With a heavy sigh, he began the next part about magicians and very unexcitedly pretended to cast spells around us, but that didn't stop

Krishna and me from acting like wonders were happening all around us.

We all laughed so hard that we could see students from the study hall room trying to peer at us from inside to see what was so much fun.

"See! That wasn't so bad. Learning is only boring if we let it be boring. Shall we continue?"

A touch of hesitation remained, but I could see they were slightly more interested now. I was surprised they had joined me so easily. Just a few minutes prior, they had hated this poem until we gave it life. Inspiring them was proving to inspire me.

Without being asked, he acted out his paragraph as he read.

Even Nelson joined in enthusiastically, and the three of us nearly died of laughter afterward.

The hesitation, nervousness, and stammering all disappeared when they were having fun. They just needed something fun to encourage them to continue. They weren't behind in the curriculum; they were just bored.

A few weeks later, Nissy Miss asked me to meet her in her office after first period. Even though I wasn't a student and hadn't done anything wrong, the idea of having to go to the principal's office still filled me with fear.

I knocked on the door. "Nissy Miss?"

"Jurnee! Come in." She cleared her desk to make an empty spot in front of the chair across from her. "We need a favor from you."

"*We?*"

"The teachers and I. Exams are coming up soon, and we were hoping that you could help us type the question papers."

I thought for a moment. Question papers must be the exams themselves. "Sure, I'd love to help."

"Great! Could you start today, instead of attending your classes for the rest of the day? We need them to be completed soon."

"No problem."

She pulled an inch-thick stack of handwritten papers onto her desk.

I could feel my eyes bulging. "Can I use a computer here? I don't think we have a printer in the hostel."

"Of course." She walked me to the secretary's computer. "We have Microsoft Word, and this is our printer. If you have any questions, just ask me or whoever is here."

"Will I be in the way of Ajitha Miss though?"

"No, no. She doesn't use the computer, so no issues."

The space was cramped with both of us, myself sitting at the computer against the wall and she to my left, sitting at the desk.

It was now time to dig into the giant stack of papers. It wasn't difficult. The majority were questions asking the student to fill in the blank or select one of the multiple-choice options. Some were more difficult to type, like the science ones where I had to use Paint to draw the shapes of different cells, or LKG questions that required me locating clip art from the preloaded gallery, since there wasn't an internet connection.

I was so engulfed in typing that I hadn't noticed a small crowd gathering.

"Jurnee Miss! How did you learn to type so fast?" A group of students were ogling from behind the window.

I continued typing as I turned to reply the student standing outside the grated window. "This isn't very fast." I had been typing since I was in third grade and did over ninety-five words per minute on average, according to a typing test we took in high school.

"And you're typing without looking! How?"

The ruckus had caused even more to gather. Students and teachers alike all came to watch the show.

"Jurnee Miss," Naveen's familiar voice came from the crowd. "How is it possible?"

"Many years of practice." I turned to him as I typed the papers.

Just then, Nissy came from her office. "All of you, go to class. Go now." As they slowly dispersed, she expressed concern. "Be careful that they don't try to distract you to see the answers."

I hadn't even thought of that. They had probably just come to catch a glimpse of their exams.

"Jurnee, don't forget that tomorrow will be class photos. Smitha Miss has brought a saree for you to wear." She saw the worried look in my eyes. "Don't take tension. We will come to dress you again."

"Thank you so much for your help. I could never do it without you."

She was my favorite person—kind, gentle, strong. She was a great leader, and I had tremendous respect for her.

The next day, she did everything she could to make me look perfect. She borrowed jewelry from the girls in the hostel and even a *bindi* from a student. She was my fairy godmother—well, maybe fairy god*sister*.

"Why do you wear less ornaments always?" she asked. "Are you Pentecostal?"

School pictures were done differently than they were back home. Instead of each student posing individually, they were taken class by class. We started with the younger students, so they wouldn't spoil their hair and uniforms, and worked our way up.

When it reached the tenth class, Raina Miss teased them. "I think the boys have spent more time combing their hair than the girls."

Her comment was met with giggles from the girls and annoyed stares from the boys. They all looked so nice though, the boys with their perfectly combed back hair, the girls with their long hair in two oiled braids. They looked so grown up yet so young at the same time.

That weekend, Joseph surprised us by allowing us to walk to a nearby place to swim. It felt a bit odd to be swimming in leggings and a t-shirt, but it was clear that anything less would not mesh with the cultural standards.

"Jurnee," Joseph began, "this water is filthy. Do not submerge your head under any circumstances."

It started off fun, all of us jumping and playing, but then I decided to go off on my own to see if I still knew how to swim. It had been ages since I'd been swimming, despite recently visiting two beaches, and I just wanted to try. As I swam to the rope, it didn't take long to remember how. Sure, it was only a doggy paddle, but it still counted.

I swam up and down the rope a few times before I noticed my arm. There was so much dirt in the water that it had attached to my arm hairs, and I could see them undulating below the water's surface.

Maliha came from behind. "Jurnee Miss …" She struggled to stay above the water.

I had just remembered how to swim; I didn't know how to save anyone.

She panicked as she grabbed onto me for balance, but this also forced me to go down as well.

I couldn't breathe. I couldn't see. I could only hear her gasps and feel her grabbing my shoulders, desperate to stay afloat. No one else had gone this far out. I didn't even know if anyone else knew how to swim. This was how it would end. I heard muffled shouting as I closed my eyes to avoid getting dirt in my contacts. If I miraculously lived, I didn't want this pair to be ruined.

Out of nowhere, I felt the weight of a flailing seventh grader coming off me. I felt hands pulling me onto a pool ring as I coughed the dirty water and opened my eyes. Akhil. He had been playing on a pool float and had maneuvered himself to the water's edge to try to save me. He was only in seventh grade and had saved my life. Genuinely saved my life.

Joseph and Rizwan immediately led the way back to the hostel. They were scolding Maliha, and I walked ahead to defend her. She hadn't done it maliciously; it was an unfortunate mistake, nothing more.

It turned out that she hadn't realized I was swimming, so she came to hang out since I was alone. By the time she had realized I was swimming and her feet no longer touched the bottom, it was too late and she panicked. She was upset enough; there was no reason to punish her.

"Maliha, I'm so sorry that happened. Are you okay?"

She stopped walking as she turned to me, wiping her eyes. "No. I'm sorry, Jurnee Miss. I almost killed you."

"No, you didn't. Everything turned out okay." I couldn't help but to hug her. I could see the stares from the other hostel students. If I showed by example I wasn't upset, maybe the others would follow suit.

Akhil, on the other hand, was declared a hero. They carried him to the hostel, and it was well deserved. I didn't get a chance to speak with him as we returned, because everyone cheered for him, but I gave him one of my hidden Dairy Milks that night. I owed my life to him; the least I could do was to give him a chocolate bar.

That night after dinner, Joseph had to attend some business, and we all went outside. Sajith and Vivek had to study for their tenth exams, and some students used my phone to call their parents, since the hostel phone only accepted incoming calls. The rest of us played tag in the dark.

The air was fresh. The sky was clear. The stars were huge. This was my home. I had even started to like having rice for almost every meal and learned that it makes a weak glue if you mash it up. Chasing each other in the dark, giggles and shouts were aplenty. Even Rizwan and Cook Auntie joined us.

All too soon, we heard tires on gravel then saw headlights. Joseph had come. There was shouting and running. I didn't have my phone and had no idea what time it was.

I shouted into the dark, "Keep my phone on the stairs!"

I made sure everyone got inside before I did. I was the foreigner so they were a bit more lenient with me. The kids would get in trouble for being out this late; Rizwan and Cook Auntie could also face consequences.

I opened the door, saw my phone on the stairs, and began walking toward it just as I heard the familiar call from Joseph as he closed his car door. "Jurnee! What is happening? I saw students running everywhere and one holding a phone. Is this what happens while I am not here?"

Shit. I was in heaps of trouble now. I waited by the door, prepared to accept the consequences.

He leaned in to whisper, "I'm not angry. I'm only strict because their parents want me to be. They're good kids. We just need to keep them safe and steer them in the right direction."

He was right. My purpose here was to teach and to be another guide and mentor for them, not to be their classmate. I was supposed to be the adult in the situation. I apologized and walked to my room, collecting my phone on the way. I felt awful.

CHAPTER 11

The next few days passed too quickly, and, before I knew it, it was my last day.

I had gone to Dhanya Supermarket the night before to buy enough Oreos to distribute to all the students today. The clerk had been so confused about why I wanted to buy dozens of sleeves of Oreos, and I chuckled to myself, thinking about the situation from her perspective. If some random American had come into my shop, asking to buy hundreds of Oreos, I would have probably been equally confused.

I waited upstairs until I heard everyone finish their breakfasts. I'd always hated crying in front of people, and now was certainly no exception. The last thing I needed was puffy panda eyes before my last day. "You can do this, Jurnee," I told myself. And I half believed it. Maybe not quite half, like a quarter. No. I twenty percent believed that I could do this.

With a deep breath, I gathered my notebook, the flash cards that I had borrowed the first day, the giant shopping bag full of Oreo packets, and the padlock. Walking downstairs, I looked out the window overlooking all the rubber trees. I looked at the photo of Joseph's father on the staircase wall. I looked at the giant statue of Jesus on the table. I looked at the foyer full of my friends in their school uniforms, a sea of blues ready for school.

A few of them shouted for me to come wait with them, but I smiled and told them I'd not yet eaten as I entered the study hall room. I saw the office, Joseph's room, Karthik's room, and Cook Auntie's room. This would be the last time I'd walk this hall on the way to breakfast before school. How had everything come to an end so soon?

A warmth grew behind my eyes. *No. No. No. Do not cry.* I looked upward and patted my lower eyelid with my shirt sleeve to preventatively absorb any stray tears.

Cook Auntie sat alone, eating in the study hall. She looked up and smiled as she motioned for me to come.

I told her, via charades, that I'd take my food and come.

Cook Auntie was a special woman. Though we didn't understand each other and had never spoken to one another, she had taken care of me as though I was her own, and I hoped she would remember me as fondly as I would remember her. She possessed a very kind and loving nature to such a degree that was so genuine and warm that when you came across it, you never wanted to leave it.

As I entered the kitchen, she immediately rose to stop me, so she could serve my food. I tried to tell her that I could manage, but she wouldn't allow me. She prepared a plate for me and carried it to the study hall room, so I filled a glass of water and followed.

As we set the items on the table across from each other, Cook Auntie embraced me in a giant hug, a hug for which I had not been quite prepared.

The warmth of the tears returned, and I felt them stream down my face, quickly at first then gradually slower.

She wiped my eyes and sat me beside her. With her own hands, Cook Auntie began to feed me.

At first, I felt foolish—an adult woman holding a college degree sitting crying while being hand fed at a breakfast table in another country. But then, I let it go. Moments like this were fleeting, and I wanted to spend as much time as I could with everyone.

When Cook Auntie had finished feeding me, I drank my water and hugged her. "I'll never forget you," I whispered into her shoulder.

She hugged me a little tighter and said something in Malayalam.

I took my dishes to the kitchen to wash them. I waved goodbye to her as I collected my things and quickly checked my phone camera to see if my mascara had spread and how red my face was before heading to school.

I knew I was late, but I also knew it didn't matter. It was the last day.

Walking through the doors, I tried to savor everything—the divots on the concrete floor, the yellowy-beige paint on the walls, the width of the pillars, the students' artwork, the smiling faces running with their bags and water bottles, the teachers in their oversized white button-up shirts covering the beautiful sarees beneath. How did a place so different from everything

I'd known come to feel more like home than any place I'd ever been? The warm feeling came again. "Hold it together, Jurnee," I scolded myself futilely.

A new idea came to mind. What if I convinced myself this wasn't the last day? Everything was normal. "You'll see everyone next week," I told myself. "And next year, you'll also come." The warmth retreated, and I relaxed my breathing as I walked to the office ahead.

As I passed the classes in session, I realized I'd missed the assembly. My last assembly. Great. I had wanted to take some photos to remember it, but I had to have my cryfest with Cook Auntie.

The students shouted to me from the windows of each class as I passed, and I waved to them, trying as hard as I could to mask any trace of sadness. It wasn't as if anyone had died.

Nissy and Ajitha Miss met me as I entered the office.

I handed the flash cards to Nissy and thanked her for allowing me to borrow them.

"The pleasure is ours, dear. Today we have quite the program planned."

"Program?"

"Yes. We've been preparing a surprise for some time. You didn't think we would just have you leave in silence, did you?"

I blushed and looked down as I tried to fight off tears. "You really didn't have to."

"It is our pleasure, Miss," Ajitha Miss chimed in.

I heard hundreds of footsteps as the students were released from their classes. They exited the front doors and sat together on the steps, row by row, class by class. Some benches had been placed at the top of the steps to add more seating. Some of the students were wearing their Annual Day dresses, and a few chairs had been lined at the front of the crowd.

Nissy guided me to the chairs, and I sat with her, Smitha, Joseph, and a few other notable guests.

Before we began, I mentioned to Nissy Miss that I had brought Oreos for the students.

"I'll call their class teachers to come and distribute them for you."

"No ... I'd like to give them out, if it's okay."

She looked to me with a loving surprise and nodded that it was okay to pass them out myself.

Walking among the rows, I handed an Oreo to each student as I tried to not cry. With each passing student, I wasn't sure if it was the last time I'd see them this closely.

Finally, the program began with a couple dance performances I remembered from Annual Day. The younger kids looked so cute in their colorful dresses, and their ability to keep the steps was impressive. Being up close really allowed me to appreciate their talent much more than I had during Annual Day. We clapped and some of them hugged me before sitting.

Several of the hostel students stood and walked to the front.

Are they going to give a speech? I wondered, trying to think what they could be doing for the program.

They got into their positions and stood, waiting. Music played, and they began a fast, modern-style dance.

Don't cry. Do not cry. You'll still be here next week, and even next year you'll come. Don't cry. This isn't the last day. This is a performance for someone's birthday. I tried anything to stop them from flowing and somehow succeeded. The dance finished, and I heartily clapped for them. They did so well, but how did they practice when I was always with them? I was amazed.

As they sat, some other students made a line at the front of the crowd. Each held a single piece of paper—notes written in my honor.

"Dear, Jurnee Miss. We are very sad that you will be going from our school."

"Madam, we were very happy to have you in our school for the last few months. We enjoyed your company, and we will always remember your smiling face. We wish you good luck and God's blessing throughout your life. We hope to see you again. Good luck, Jurnee Miss."

"I like Jurnee Ma'am very much. I am so sad you was going from this school. I am so fear to talk to she. I am saying thank you for spend this day with us. I talk to she that time I got so many new English words. We love you very much."

"Our dear most Jurnee Miss. We all love you very much. We are proud to be your students. You teach us very well. We all glad you are here. You are our's friend also. Thank you for spending the time with us. When you come here, we study about English grammar. Happy journey to our dear most Jurnee Mam. You play with us and enjoy with."

"I would like to say a few words about our dearest Jurnee Miss. She has always been a teacher, a friend, and a true guidance for us in all our problems. In this end, I want to say, I enjoyed a heck of time. Let us preserve this treasured memories."

"Dear, Jurnee Ma'am. I like you very much. You are looking like Barbie. I will missing you so much. Thank you for playing with us. I am so sad you are going."

"We are so sad, because you are going, but you are a best teacher. We are requested you to come back to our school, because we love you."

"I like you very much. You looking like a Barbie doll. I like your eyes very much. I like your character very much. Thank you for spending time with me. I will miss you."

With each student, I lost more and more control.

When they finished, they brought their handwritten speeches and carefully drawn pictures to me.

In that moment, I decided to keep them forever. After receiving dozens of heartfelt notes and speeches, it was time for performances.

There were a couple more dances, but, from nowhere, a car approached the gate, and whispers erupted throughout the crowd of students. The car pulled through the gate, and some of them stood to get a better look. What was happening? Who was that?

A tall man stepped from the car with large potato sacks. The potato sacks moved, and every urge to cry stopped; my urge to be terrified set in. What was inside? He pulled two metal sticks with hooks on them from his car. The driver brought out some clear boxes containing snakes. Were snakes in the bags too? Who was this guy? How did everyone know him? Were these snakes poisonous?

Joseph walked to the microphone to give the announcement and welcome him. I would finally know who he was. The announcement, however, was in Malayalam.

Luckily, Ananya saw me confused and came quickly to my side. "He is Vava Suresh, snake master. He has captured more than one hundred king cobra snakes."

The color drained from my face, and my muscles stiffened. Did he bring a king cobra to a school?

I had been sitting behind the microphone but moved to sit with the students. It was partially to get a better view, partially to sit with my friends one last time, but mostly to get away from the snakes.

One by one, he brought them out of the bags and the boxes. He held them with the metal hooks, and he even kissed the back of the head of a king cobra—an actual king cobra. It was terrifying, and I stopped breathing as he brought the snake closer to his face. He had such great control over the snakes, and it was no wonder why he was so revered among the students and teachers.

While the teachers and older students ran to take selfies with him after he had finished, I played the hand clap game with some third-grade girls. When I had taught it to them, I hadn't done it in several years and I was shocked when they picked it up so quickly and enjoyed it as much as they did. I wasn't sure if I would ever have the opportunity to do this again.

Rizwan came behind where we were sitting and gave me two books. I opened them and saw every student's contact information. They had been circulating and collecting each other's information, so I could stay in touch with everyone. There were personal messages and many saying they would add me on Facebook as soon as the term ended and they could use their phones again.

The rest of the day seemed to fly by. Dinner had finished, and we sat around the study hall room, chatting. The kids took turns asking what I would do when I got home and if my family missed me. I answered all their questions but couldn't focus. I'd never been so sad to leave a place in my life.

"You know one thing?" I started.

"No, miss. Tell us," one boy in the back called out.

"Stars back home are nothing compared to these."

"You have different stars?"

"No, no. But yours look so much bigger and brighter. I've never seen anything so beautiful."

We decided to enjoy them one more time as all of us walked to the basketball court. Would this be the last time we were all together? I laid down to look at the stars that I might never see again, and also to hide the fact I was near sobbing. The others followed suit and looked up. I quickly glanced around to make sure the boys and girls were lying separately, since I was supposed to be responsible.

"Jurnee Miss?" a small voice called from a few feet away.

"Mm?"

"Don't go."

"I don't want to," I said as I lost all control in holding back my tears.

"We love you, miss," one said to me, then other voices echoed the same.

"I love you guys too." My voice broke; my cover was blown. Shit.

"Don't cry, *na*. Call the airplane company and change the ticket or come back next year. MD will definitely allow you to come back."

Several of them had come to my side, now in a giant bear hug. I didn't want to go home. We sat there for a moment, taking in our last time together, and I noticed a couple of them crying also. I never imagined they would miss me as much as I would miss them.

We spent some more time together, cuddling in silence, before Rizwan told us it was time to sleep. At his prompting, we groaned in protest but headed to our respective rooms.

Once inside, I tried to scroll through Facebook for a distraction. I couldn't believe my last day at the school was done. I didn't know when I'd see them again after today. I called Anooj.

"Jurnee?"

"Hey, how's it going?"

"I am fine. How are you?"

"I don't want to go."

He laughed. "I don't think *anyone* wants you to go."

"But, really. I don't feel ready. I don't feel like I'm meant to go."

"You can always stay. The school will take you, or you can stay with my family even. If you want to be in Kerala, we can find a way."

"My family would kill me though."

"Follow your heart, *da*. People move long distances quite often to join the military or a fancy college across the country or take their dream job in a big city."

"Maybe you're right. I'll call Air India in the morning."

"Jurnee?"

"Anooj?" I mocked him in the same tone.

"Get some rest. I don't want you to be asleep this time tomorrow when I see you."

"*Fiiiine.* Goodnight."

"Goodnight, Jurnee Miss."

I had really grown to enjoy his company. There was no way I could have handled everything here without him guiding me and explaining things. Because of him, I had even been able to help another foreigner better adjust to things here. I had grown so much in just a few months. It was unbelievable.

I called Air India first thing the next morning. I *had* to extend my flight. This couldn't be the end. But, due to the late notice, the charge to reschedule the flight was 40,000 rupees. That was more than $500. I didn't have $500. I mean, I had credit cards, but that was hardly the same, and I didn't want to go into debt when I didn't even have a job.

I sat back on the bed and cried. This was really goodbye. This tiny bed, my desk with the plastic floral table cover, my tiny mirror over the sink, the view of the neighbor's yard from my window, it was all over.

"Jurnee Miss?" Devu called out. "Come for breakfast. It's getting late."

"Sure, okay. One second," I replied as I wiped my eyes and checked my face in the mirror. This was my last day. I couldn't waste it crying all the time by myself.

We all sat with the tables joined together as we ate our *idli* and chickpea curry. It was one of my favorite meals we had been having, and I would miss this so much—homemade, healthy food every meal surrounded by kids who had transformed from my students to my friends.

Joseph made an exception to allow the boys upstairs as everyone came to my room to help me pack. Some of them seemed just as sad as me. With all my anxiety and self-doubt, it was a relief to know I meant to them at least some of what they meant to me.

Joseph and I had also arranged for me to go off campus with a couple students to bring pizza for lunch. They had all been wanting to try it, and a Domino's had just opened nearby; it was perfect timing for my last meal here.

Nehemiah arrived in his small red car and, joined with Karthik and Akhil, we set off for Kollam. It was about an hour drive, and they chatted in Malayalam the whole way, but I didn't mind. I was looking at my village, taking mental notes of every last tree and goat.

The hour flew by, and soon we arrived. A few doors down from Domino's was KFC. Karthik and Akhil were dying to try it, so we had a snack before we picked up the pizza. They split a bucket of chicken, and I had a veggie burger, but Nehemiah said he didn't want anything. After the three of us begged him to try something, he settled for the cheapest thing on the menu—the thirty-rupees veggie burger that I had also gotten. He hated it, but Karthik and Akhil loved their bucket.

After we finished, we pick up the pizza from Domino's. The total bill came to over 8,000 rupees, more than $100 in pizza.

Every worker turned to the front to see what fool had spent a month's salary just on pizza. When they realized I was a foreigner, I could see they still thought I was foolish, but they shrugged it off.

We had ordered pizzas, garlic bread, and enough chocolate lava cakes for everyone. I was so excited to see them try it for the first time as we got into the car to go to the hostel. But we weren't going in the right direction. I wasn't certain it was the wrong direction, but I trusted them, so I didn't say anything.

It wasn't long before we pulled up to a beach. Nehemiah said something to the boys in Malayalam, and they relayed it to me.

"Jurnee Miss, we cannot stay long, because no one knows that we are here. He just wanted to let you visit the beach once."

I couldn't help but to smile to myself. I had now visited more beaches in India than I had back home in the US. We sat on a rock toward the back of the sand as we each ate a piece of pizza and some garlic bread. We even opened one of the lava cakes and split it. I made note that this one was mine, so they could still enjoy another back at the hostel.

This beach was just like the others; no one actually got in the water. We chatted a little bit but not much, mostly just for them to comment how much they liked the pizza. They didn't even say much in Malayalam. We just wanted to spend time together.

After a little while, Nehemiah stood, indicating it was time to return. I was that much closer to getting home, and my heart got that much heavier. The ride back went too fast. It felt like it was just five minutes, even though I knew it had been about an hour.

Arriving at the hostel with everyone running toward the car reminded me of the first time I had gotten here. Krishna reached for pizza boxes, and everyone else clamored to get a view of what we brought. We had come full circle.

Cook Auntie was the most intrigued. She carefully opened the box, like it may contain a bomb, and smelled it closely. Only a few had eaten pizza before, and the rest were dying to try some.

Half of them liked the pizza, none of them liked the garlic bread, but all of them liked the chocolate lava cake. The funny thing was they were shocked to see me eating with my hands after all the struggle I had with it at dinner.

"We always eat pizza with our hands," I explained. I briefly remembered deep-dish pizza but didn't want to go into a half-hour lecture about different pizza styles.

"Jurnee Miss, are you going to miss our Kerala food?" Naveen asked.

"I am."

"But I think you are happy to not have rice anymore."

"I actually quite like rice now. I'll really miss it. And don't call me *Miss*."

"Why not, Jurnee Miss?" Sachin asked.

"I'm not your teacher anymore. Yesterday was my last day at school, so now we are friends only."

"Ok, *Jurnee*," they said in hushed tones, like they were worried they may be caught.

My phone rang. It was Anooj. That meant he was here, and I wasn't ready for this. I could feel the air escaping my lungs. This was it. It was all over now.

"Jurnee Miss, who was that?" Naveen asked.

I glared at him jokingly.

"Okay. *Jurnee*, who was that?"

"It's my friend Anooj. He's here to take me to the airport."

"No, Jurnee. You don't want to go." They protested one by one.

I couldn't hold it back anymore; I started to cry.

A few of them cried also.

"I have to, um, I have to get my bags." I had to stop crying in front of them. I was making myself look like a fool.

They followed me up the stairs and carried my bags to the foyer.

I handed the padlock to Joseph.

"You're always welcome, Jurnee. We will miss you here," Joseph said. "Tell your parents I said hello and that they've raised a wonderful daughter."

Smitha leaned over to hug me. "Please come back anytime."

"We all love you, dear. Come soon," Nissy said with a hug.

"Thank you so much for allowing me to come. I've loved my time here so much. I'll miss you all too." *Do not cry. Do not cry. Do not cry.* "I'll do my best to return."

The three of them sat at the foyer table as the students and I walked through the front doors for the last time.

I almost cried until I saw Anooj. At least these next few hours wouldn't be completely unbearable. I tried to smile at him, but I couldn't bring myself to all the way.

As we got closer, Anooj opened the trunk, and he and Vivek put in my luggage. I hugged everyone and tried not to cry. It was a miserable attempt.

When I reached Sindhu—she was the last one—I hugged her a little tighter.

"You don't want to cry, miss. Be happy. You are going to America." She offered the end of her black scarf for me to wipe my eyes.

"Smile, Jurnee," Naveen commanded.

They put my backpack in the back seat, and I reluctantly sat in the passenger seat. I realized I hadn't said even a word to Anooj, but how could I say hello when I was in the midst of one of the hardest goodbyes?

I waved to them as we pulled away slowly.

They followed us to the gate, and seeing some of them start to cry made me cry again too. We crossed the gate, and I waved to the students and to the security guard. This was it. It was all over.

"Jurnee Miss, did someone die?" Anooj teased me.

"Ha. Ha. Very funny," I said, mildly annoyed.

"You'll see them again, and everyone has Facebook now. Don't worry."

He was right. He smiled as he gently squeezed my hand.

Everything would be fine.

CHAPTER 12

There wasn't much time, so we had a quick dinner of a *McAloo* from Indian McDonald's as we headed toward the airport.

"I'm really going to miss you, Jurnee."

I smiled and looked down. I would miss him, my students and colleagues, Kerala, everything. It took every ounce of strength to not cry again. "I'll miss you too. Thank you so much for everything you've done to help me the past couple months. I couldn't have done it without you."

He smiled the biggest smile I'd seen on him, but a certain sadness reflected in his eyes I didn't quite understand. It couldn't possibly be because I was leaving. We'd only known each other for a short while, though I did consider him a good friend. I wondered if we would lose touch when I got back to my real life.

We drove in silence. This was all going too fast. I was heading home and would have to start the process of applying for jobs all over again. I would be jetlagged. I might have to sit next to an annoying person for twelve hours.

"Everything okay?"

It wasn't. "Of course!"

We pulled into the airport. It was even less okay.

He parked the car and turned to me. "Very well. Shall I get your bags?"

I nodded, but I didn't want to go. It felt like everything was happening in double speed, and, before I knew it, we were at the front door.

The guard totted a massive gun, and I turned to Anooj for confirmation that this was normal. Was there some present danger I should be aware of?

He nodded that Indian nod to tell me it was okay. He stepped to close the gap between us and hugged me tightly into his chest. There was no way I would have been able to do all of this without him.

I hugged him back tightly, breathing him in, ignoring the stares of unapproving passersby. The hug continued as neither of us were sure when to let go. But I knew it was getting late, and I should check in. I released the grip of my arms, and he followed my lead, wiping a tear from my eye. One thing I'd learned today was my tear ducts were not at all obedient when I told them to stop.

With my bags, ticket print-out, and passport in hand, we approached the security guard. He would only allow ticketholders to enter. Anooj and I exchanged glances, and I walked to the check in as I turned back to wave goodbye.

I looked back on all the memories, all the fears I'd overcome. I had gone to a strange place where I knew no one. I had made friends. I had finally gotten to teach. I gave a speech in front of a thousand people. *A thousand people.* And I had met Anooj. I could have been assigned to any Uber driver, but I got him. So much had happened that I didn't even feel like the same person anymore.

I hoped I could stay in touch with all the kids and teachers during summer break, maybe even after. I felt so sad to leave them but so happy to have all our memories. I made a mental note that I absolutely must return, even if not soon. I couldn't just not see them all again.

As I walked to check in my bag, I noticed everyone but me was excited to be here. I wondered where they were going—maybe on vacation or moving for a new job or to study. Maybe they were going home too. Why was I so sad to go home?

It was finally my turn in line as I lifted my bag onto the scale and gave my passport to the attendant.

"Trivandrum to Chicago via Dubai?" she confirmed.

"Yes."

"Actually, this flight had been cancelled. We have placed you on the next flight."

Did I hear that right? "I'm sorry, what?"

"The flight was cancelled. You will be on the next flight at twelve fifteen." She returned my passport to me over the table.

I couldn't believe it. Was I dreaming? Had this actually happened? "Are you sure?"

She was annoyed now. "Yes. I am sure. Now please make way for the next person in line."

"Thank you." I was too happy to notice how rude she had been. This was perfect.

I texted Anooj to let him know I wasn't leaving for a few hours. I had three more hours before I had to be back at the airport, and I wanted to do everything. Luckily, I had a five-hour layover in Dubai, so I probably wouldn't miss the connecting flight. Everything had worked out seamlessly.

As I walked outside, I saw Anooj approaching me. "So, what do you want to do for the next three hours?" he asked as he lifted my bag into the trunk. Neither of us could conceal joy that we had more time together.

"I want to eat everything."

"Your wish is my command, madam," he teased as he opened my door with a bow. For a moment, it seemed as though he was even happier than me.

"I know exactly what I want."

"To be kidnapped?" he teased.

Yes, please. "*Vada*."

"Street or restaurant?"

"Street. Street. Street." This was my last chance.

"Are you sure you want to take the risk? What if you get sick right before your flight?"

"I'll be fine. Promise."

He looked to me with more than a hint of concern. "Are you sure?"

"Positive. How can I leave without it?"

He laughed as we spotted a street vendor with a line. I remembered the lesson he had taught me about how I should only buy street food if there was a line. It meant it was good and fresh, that I could watch it being cooked to ensure hygiene, and that it didn't contain raw ingredients.

The stand was packed, and everyone stared at me. I had been at the school so long that people had stopped staring at me for the most part, but no one here knew me. I was a stranger, and I felt like a zoo animal again.

Anooj noticed my discomfort. "Do you want to eat in the car?"

"No, it's fine. They have a bench," I said with a weak smile as I nervously looked at all of the eyes scrutinizing me.

Every bit of discomfort I had faded away when it was our turn to get the *vada*. He paid the owner as we got four *vada*. It came with my favorite tomato chutney and even coconut chutney on a small plastic red plate. I couldn't wait to start eating until we had sat down.

"Hungry?"

"Of course," I said, mouth full, trying to ignore everyone staring at me while I ate.

"They just want to know if you like it or not. Our food is very precious to us." It was like he always knew exactly what I was thinking.

Knowing it was my last few hours and no longer caring what anyone thought, I turned to the gawking crowd. "Your *vada* is delicious. I prefer tomato chutney to coconut chutney. Please stop staring. Your queries have been answered."

Anooj couldn't control his laughter, and, as soon as he started, I couldn't help but start too. We immediately soaked the remaining two *vada* in chutney, returned the plate to the owner, and ran to the car, laughing all the way.

"What happened back there?" he asked.

"I'm just so tired of being stared at. It felt so freeing to finally say something. I just wish they knew how it feels to be stared at all the time by everyone."

"I know. How about this? I won't look at you for the rest of the night." He covered his eyes with his hand.

With a roll of my eyes, I pulled his hand off his face. "You're *sooo* funny."

"Where to next, madam?"

"I want *dosa*."

"You just had *vada*."

"*Dosa. Dosa. Dosa.* The thinnest, crispiest, oiliest *dosa* in all Trivandrum."

"*Dosa* it is," he said as he opened my car door.

I was going to eat everything in this entire town before my flight.

We finally made it to a small restaurant and had *dosa* as long as my arm. It was the best *dosa* I'd ever had, but I was getting full. I didn't want to get full. I wanted to keep eating and eating. I wanted to remember every morsel, every taste, every smell. With each minute, it was slipping further away.

"Now what?"

"I need *chaiyya*."

"*Chaiyya* it is." He raised his arm with one finger in the air to call the waiter.

I took the small metal tumbler in my hands and breathed in the aroma. I wished there was an equivalent of photos for all the senses. I didn't want to just remember what I saw. I wanted to remember how it smelled and tasted. I even wanted to remember the humidity and the honking.

I usually waited a while to drink it, since *chaiyya* was served so hot, but, since Anooj had started drinking his, I thought maybe it had cooled. It hadn't. I forgot Indians seemed to have iron throats and could consume even the hottest of liquids, but it burned my throat and coughed.

"Are you okay?" he asked, concerned.

"I'm fine. It's just hot."

"So, what do you want to do after this?" he asked as he motioned to the waiter to bring the little metal bowl used to pour the tea back and forth to cool it faster.

I checked my phone. It was almost eight, just one hour left before I had to go to the airport.

"Jurnee? What happened?"

"It's almost over."

"It's not over. You'll visit again."

"I know." My cheeks grew warm again. I was going to cry. If people weren't staring enough before, this would certainly make them stare even more.

"It looks like you need dessert."

He was right. "What do you have in mind? I haven't had any sweets here, just Dairy Milk and Dark Fantasy and plum cake."

"Let's go and have my favorite."

"Which one?"

"Would you know what it was even if I told you the name?"

I couldn't help but to laugh. He was right.

Anooj paid the man at the counter on the way out, and we got back into the car.

After driving for a few minutes, we arrived at a shop with a big black sign with white letters: *Sri Krishna Sweets.* It sounded promising. As we approached the door, I glanced at my phone—8:15. With a deep breath, I followed Anooj inside. This was our last stop.

He immediately went to the long display counters featuring dozens of different sweets, none of which I had ever seen or heard of before. I wanted to try all of them, but I didn't want to get a stomachache.

Anooj called the attendant and said something in Malayalam that resulted in a small sample of a white rectangle. He took one for himself and handed the other to me. "*Mysore Pak*," he announced as he ate his. "This is my favorite."

It was soft and melted in my mouth. It was like butter and milk had a delicious semisolid baby. My enthusiasm must have been obvious because he asked me if I wanted another. As I had my second sampling, he asked what I wanted to try next.

Looking down the row of sweets, I saw another that looked like a flaky brown cube. "This one," I said with a point.

"Ah, *Soan Papdi*. Great choice."

It melted like cotton candy but had nuts and an aftertaste reminiscent of Fruity Pebbles. It was incredible.

"Now what?"

Were we going to eat everything? "That one." I pointed to one that looked like peanut brittle.

"*Chikki*," he said. "Another good choice."

"Are there any bad choices?" I teased as he handed me the sample. It tasted so similarly to peanut brittle, and it was absolutely delicious.

"Last one is my choice," he declared. "Close your eyes."

I closed my eyes and heard him make a request to the counter person.

"Now open your mouth."

I hadn't been hand fed in my life as much as I had been hand fed whilst I was in Kerala. It was delicious though. It was soft and extremely sweet.

"This is *Tirunelveli halwa*," he informed.

"No."

He looked confused.

"It's not *truvineli halwa*. It's heaven."

He laughed at my awful pronunciation. "So, which one do you want to take home with you? My treat."

I recalled the four we had tried. *Chikki* I could basically get at home. The *halwa* was good but not the best of the four. The *Soan Papdi* was good, but I didn't really like nuts that much. "*Mysore Pak*."

His eyes lit up. "My favorite is your favorite too, *aa*?"

I smiled as he placed the order to the man behind the counter, until I heard the quantity. "Did you just say one kg, as in kilogram, as in, like, two pounds? Isn't that a lot?"

"You'll eat some and remember us. You'll share some with your friends and your family as you tell them stories of your time here. It won't go to waste."

I smiled as he handed me the box. The smile lasted until I checked my phone again—8:50.

"Is it time?" he asked, but he didn't need to. He could always read me as easily as I could read a clock.

We walked to the car. It was the last time I would be sitting in his car. It was the last time I would see the city and these trees. I tried to not be heartbroken. It wasn't the last time. I would return to see my students, my village, and Anooj.

Before I knew it, we had reached the airport. I got out of the car for the last time. He retrieved my bag for the last time. I strapped on my backpack for the last time. He walked me to the doors for the last time, past the guard with the giant gun for the last time. He hugged me goodbye, and I looked at the trees for the last time, feeling the air for the last time.

What was meant to just be a minute to say goodbye was much longer. We stood there, neither wanting to let go. Letting go meant not knowing when we would see each other again. He had become one of my best friends in such a short period of time. This time, he was the first to let go.

He bent down and whispered, "I don't want you to get tensed or risk being late. As much as you will miss us, your family misses you more. You should go to them."

With tears in my eyes, I nodded and walked inside. I was struck again by how happy everyone looked and how unhappy I felt. Soon it was my turn, and I gave my passport to the clerk as I lifted my bag onto the scale.

"You're late," she said sharply as she printed my boarding pass and stamped it.

As I walked to security, the boarding announcement played over the intercom. Luckily, I wasn't in the first group, so I had time to make it through. They let me keep on my shoes and keep the liquids inside my backpack as I set it on the conveyer belt and approached the women's line. I had found it strange at first, but now I really appreciated the separate line and the privacy while they wanded us.

She smiled as she stamped my boarding pass and allowed me to proceed.

I collected my bag and reached my gate just as they announced my boarding section. The good thing about being late was that the wait wasn't as long. I stood in line, holding my passport as I waited to board.

"Did you enjoy our Kerala?" a random man in the line asked me.

"I loved it." I smiled as I held back tears.

We shuffled into the flight, and I sat. Checking my phone as I waited, I saw two emails and a WhatsApp message.

I opened the first email. It was from Joseph. *Thank you for all the work you did for us. You are a wonderful person and a credit to the humanity. Children remember you with fondness. Thank you for your help.*

I made note in my phone memos to reply when I got home, and moved to the next message. It was from one of the schools I had applied to. *Dear, Ms. Ryan. I attempted to contact you about a recent teaching opportunity that just opened at St. Joseph Grade School, but I haven't yet heard back from you. If you have any interest, please contact me at your earliest availability. Thank you, Danielle Curtis, Principal St. Joseph Grade School.*

Oh my god. An actual interview offer? With almost the same name as my school in Kerala? This was fate. I would do everything I could to ace it.

I sent a quick message to my parents to let them know I was on the flight and checked the WhatsApp message waiting. It was Anooj. *Jurnee, I wasn't completely honest with you.*

What do you mean? I wrote.

I know that the chances are not in my favor, but I must tell you.

Tell me what?

Jurnee, he sent and nothing more. Then the heading showed he was still typing.

I braced myself. What could it possibly be? What if it was awful? I waited.

Jurnee, I love you.

I had started having feelings for him when he came for Annual Day and after he spoke with Sajith's dad to make sure I would be ok, but I never thought that it would be reciprocated so I didn't even give it a second thought before. I had no idea how to reply. I began typing a few times but kept deleting it before sending.

I know it seems sudden for you, but it is not sudden for me.

I still didn't know what to say. I liked him, but it wasn't that easy. What if I said *yes*? Our friendship would change; we would have to navigate a weird long-distance relationship; we would have to travel anytime we wanted to see each other; the time difference was basically twelve hours. It was impossible. But if I said *no*, everything would be ruined.

Don't feel pressure. Think during your flight and let me know. We can begin AnooJurnee whenever you decide.

AnooJurnee? What was that? After a moment, I understood. He tried to mash our names together, like Brangelina to make *a new journey*. It was actually pretty clever.

Whether you accept or not, you are always welcome to our Kerala. It is now your Kerala also. This is your home. Please come anytime.

A moment later, a flight attendant told me to store my phone.

I sent him a single smiling emoji as I turned off my phone and looked outside. I wanted to remember this. I wanted to remember the men in reflective vests carting around baggage. I wanted to remember the fence on the edge, and the trees just behind it. I wanted to remember the smell. Though at first overwhelming, I'd miss it. I'd miss the food, even rice. The people. The clothes. The music. The enthusiasm. The hospitality. The warmth and kindness. I'd never met so many wonderful people in all my life. I was going home, but my heart was staying behind.

I saw only clouds and my reflection in the window when I noticed I'd been crying without realizing it. Resting my head on the window, I closed my eyes and prayed I wouldn't forget these memories or any of the friends I'd made. I prayed we'd meet again, and that they'd also remember me fondly.

Before I knew it, I had drifted off to sleep.

Thank you for reading *A New Journey*.

AUTHOR'S NOTE

Back in late 2014, I stumbled upon an opportunity to volunteer teaching in Kerala. It was my third trip to India but my first time in the south and my first time in a village. I never imagined I would cherish those days even years later.

I started writing this book in 2017, because I have an awful memory. I realized these wonderful memories and anecdotal stories were slowly fading, and I wanted to remember them always, so I decided to immortalize them in a book. I also wanted to use it as a way to dispel stereotypical perceptions of India, so others could fall in love with it just as I have.

For those who follow me online, you may notice some parallels with Kannan and Anooj. This isn't at all how we met, but I wanted to weave him into Anooj, so that I can write a sequel about our wedding. Watch out for its release Valentine's Day 2021! A random man on a footpath in Bangalore did help me with an unruly auto driver once though. Each small story was inspired by true events.

Everything that happened at the school was based on my own experiences. Some were slightly dramatized; most names were changed for privacy; a few events were rearranged for flow; but overall, this is a glimpse of my life in Kerala.

I will donate a percentage of all book sales to the scholarship fund of the school where I taught. Thank you for your support.

Follow me—Quora - Samantha Kannan

Twitter - @NaanSamantha

Instagram - @SamanthaKannan

TikTok - @SamanthaKannan

YouTube - Samantha Kannan

Enjoy some photos of my trip.

1: To commemorate the start of SJIA's 13th Annual Day, flower petals were arranged on the steps of the school.

2: Visiting a nearby house in the village with some of the hostel students. From left to right: Rukmini, Arun, Aiswarya, Nandu, Vijay, Abhinav, Amarjith, Amal P, Agin, Shiva, Anju, me, Joel, the neighbor, Mohazina, Jasmine, and Femi.

3: My day on bus duty with Shyny Miss.

4: A first grade classroom.

5: Some of the hostel boys eating with spoons after I made an attempt to eat with my hand.

6: Arjun and Nandu showing me the baby pigeon upstairs.

7: The youngest of the hostel, our naughty Joel, often referred to endearingly as *achu*.

8: My farewell party at school with Nissy Miss and some students.

9: One of the many kind messages I received from my students at my farewell. I still have every one of them